Date D

Survey-Guided Development II:

A MANUAL FOR CONSULTANTS

Survey-Guided Development II:

A MANUAL FOR CONSULTANTS

(Revised Edition)

D. L. Hausser, Ph.D.
U.S. Civil Service Commission

P. A. Pecorella, Ph.D.
Consultant

A. L. Wissler, M.S.W.
University of Michigan

University Associates, Inc.
8517 Production Avenue
San Diego, California 92121

Contents

The University of Michigan's Institute for Social Research is the largest university-based research organization in the social sciences. Through its four centers and their constituent programs, it conducts basic research in psychology, sociology, economics, and political science, as well as in the applied fields of management, education, and health. Among these, the Organizational Development Research Program has, for the last decade, conducted research on such processes of organization development and change as diagnosis, model acceptance, change agentry, and evaluation of interventions.

Foreword

For nearly a decade, a steady stream of staff members have endeavored to build a systematic body of scientific knowledge concerning the organizational development process. In its first five years, this effort employed as a vehicle the Michigan Intercompany Longitudinal Study. Drawing upon the organizational writings of Rensis Likert and the survey feedback experiences of Floyd Mann, this large effort went on to produce a unique, standardized questionnaire instrument (the *Survey of Organizations*) and a bank of resulting, accumulated data surrounding intervention.

Using the data and experiences of this and subsequent periods, a body of empirical findings has been produced and conceptual statements generated which integrate those findings and experiences. The term *survey-guided development* has been applied to the whole, in recognition of the twin facts that development is at heart an adaptation process and that the survey is a guidance mechanism within that process.

From the first, however, it has been apparent to those of us responsible for the Organizational Development Research Program that a body of findings is useful only to the extent that it is transmittable. The results of research must be useable by practitioners, or they acquire little more than curiosity value.

This present manual represents an important and, in my view, successful effort to convert research findings in this field to implementable form. Those who use it will find it clear, comprehensive, and carefully sequenced. It states rationale as well as method, reasons as well as procedures. As such, it is a resource volume, a manual of requisite skills, and a practitioner's guide. It is, hopefully, the first of many.

David G. Bowers

Preface

This manual is intended as a tool for both external consultants and internal resource people who are, or will be, involved in survey-guided development. It is intended for use in two ways: initially as a self-training package and subsequently as a reference and operating guide. The goals of the manual are to provide a complete description of the survey-guided-development process as viewed and practiced by the Organizational Development Research Program and to equip consultants and resource people with the information they need to guide this development process effectively.

The manual is divided into four major sections. The first section provides an overview of survey-guided development, including the use of standardized questionnaires as a data-collection technique, and a description of the Survey of Organizations —the questionnaire presently employed by the Organizational Development Research Program. The next two sections deal with understanding survey data and utilizing these data to identify and solve problems in organizational functioning. The focus in Section 2 is on concepts and activities relevant at the work-group level. In Section 3 the focus shifts to system-level activities and concepts. These sections describe the range of things the consultant can expect to happen while working at each of these levels and provide appropriate guidelines for making interventions. Finally, Section 4 contains descriptions of consultant skills and information specifically referenced from Sections 2 and 3. It also stands on its own as a general index.

A careful reading and study of the entire manual will provide consultants and internal resource people with understanding of the survey-guided-development process as it ideally should progress. As much as possible, this process should be followed. Most situations, however, have constraints that make the ideal process difficult—and sometimes impossible—to achieve in all aspects. Consequently, it is crucial to recognize that the several activities included in survey-guided development must be adapted to fit the situational constraints that are operating. Some general guidelines for how to adapt the survey-guided-development process in less than ideal situations are provided in the manual. Obviously, specific contingencies cannot be discussed in a manual intended for use in many diverse situations. This highlights the fact that strategy planning must take place in relation to each setting.

It should also be noted that the manual in its present form does not address the issue of evaluating consultants; that is, it does not deal with techniques for assessing the skill levels of consultants. Moreover, assessing the degree to which organizational functioning changes as a result of a development effort is not discussed in depth, although some mechanisms for such assessment are built in through the cyclical nature of survey-guided development. For example, each time the survey is readministered, previous survey results provide a standard of comparison. Less explicit coverage of these evaluation issues does not imply that such processes are unimportant; rather this reflects the priority we have given to providing basic information to people who are relatively unfamiliar with this change strategy.

We wish to acknowledge at least some of the many groups and individuals who provided valuable information and support in the preparation of this manual. Our thanks go to the staff comprising the Organizational Development Research Program (ISR) under the creative guidance of David G. Bowers. In particular, thanks are due to Jerome Franklin for his helpful editorial and content critiques, and to Barbara Wank and Jane Delaney for their clerical assistance. Research for the development of an earlier version of this manual (for use in navy settings) was supported by the Bureau of Naval Personnel and conducted under the Office of Naval Research Contract No. N00014-67-A-0181-0056. Their support is gratefully acknowledged.

Section I

Theory and Measurement in Survey-Guided Development

Module 1:   What is Survey-Guided Development?

Module 2:   Using a Standardized Questionnaire:

The Survey of Organizations

Module 1:
What Is Survey-Guided Development?

This module provides the background for understanding survey-guided development. The first section includes a definition of this process and describes the importance and usage of a standardized questionnaire in assessing the present state of, as well as changes in, organizational functioning. Both the goal of improved organizational functioning and the consultant's role in reaching this goal are explored. The consultant is described as a link between information about organizational functioning, information about organizational development, and members of the organization undergoing a change. Finally, motivation is discussed as a key issue in survey-guided development.

DEFINITION OF SURVEY-GUIDED DEVELOPMENT

This module is designed to answer the question, "What is survey-guided development?" It is an important question because as someone planning to be involved in a survey-guided development effort, you are likely to be asked that question, in one form or another, over and over again. Some people may want a brief and simple answer, others may prefer a detailed explanation, and still others require something in between. After studying this module, you should have the ability to answer the question in as much or as little detail as is desired.

What is *survey-guided development?* The name itself suggests two important facets of the answer:

First, it is the *development* or improvement of the capacity of organization members to function effectively in accomplishing their day-to-day and longer range tasks.

In a truly effective organization, people at all levels of the organizational hierarchy are motivated and able to solve problems in a way that

1

anticipates and eliminates problems without creating new ones.

Second, survey-guided development utilizes a questionnaire asking for many individuals' perceptions of the aspects of organizational functioning that are most important in affecting performance, satisfaction, and motivation in organizations. By comparing perceptions of how the organization does function with some standard of how it might or should function, the areas that need development become apparent.

DIAGNOSTIC INFORMATION

An organization is not a fixed entity located in an unchanging environment. Rather, it is in constant flux with its members attempting to adapt to changing conditions both inside and outside the organization. Constructive adaptation to these changing conditions necessitates having information about how the organization is working and where there are problems in its functioning. Survey-guided development utilizes a questionnaire to efficiently provide adequate and accurate information about how the organization functions. This information provides organization members with the kind of descriptive picture that can help them to monitor and adapt to changing demands and situations more smoothly and to anticipate and solve problems more effectively.

To discuss these two points in any more detail it is necessary to understand the theory and assumptions underlying survey-guided development.

Survey-guided development is based on the theory that three factors need to be taken into account in an organization development effort: the behaviors that are problematic, the conditions that create those behaviors, and the interventions or activities that will correct the conditions creating the problems. These three factors may be stated in the form of three relatively simple questions: *What* is it that people are doing, or not doing, that is a problem? *Why* are they doing or not doing these particular things? *Which* of a large number of possible interventions or activities would be most likely to solve the problems by focusing on why the problems exist? It is crucial that these three questions be answered, and answered correctly, since it would not help the organization if the organization development effort focused on changing behaviors that were not the problem behaviors. Nor would it help if a great deal of effort went toward solving the right problems by changing the wrong conditions or by using the wrong interventions to change them. Thus, it is important that changes be based upon an accurate *diagnosis* of problems and their causes.

However, the task of formulating such a diagnosis is difficult because change in organizations involves taking into account, at one time, the appropriate behaviors and inter-relationships of many people:

- in many jobs and roles
- at various levels in the organization
- at many points in time
- under varying conditions.

How is this much information collected? In order to get accurate information for such a diagnosis, *many* people within the same organization, but in different work situations, should be asked to answer the same set of questions. Gathering multiple perceptions of the organization lessens the chance that the diagnosis will reflect organizational functioning as viewed from a few unique work situations or as distorted by individual biases. In contrast to this, if just a few people were asked to describe the organization, a very limited number of work situations and personal biases would be represented. It is highly unlikely that limited information such as this would reflect the actual state of the organization's functioning. Think of your own organization: Do you know any small group of people who could give a picture of the organization that would accurately represent its functioning at all levels in all departments regarding all their operations? The larger and the more complex the organization, the more an accurate diagnosis depends on gathering multiple perceptions.

Once multiple perceptions have been gathered, there is a need to combine and summarize them in a meaningful way so that the amount of information to be digested is not overwhelming.

This summary indicates *how* an organization is functioning. But people are probably more interested in *how well* their organization functions. This means a *standard of comparison* is needed. There are at least four kinds of comparisons that could be made:

1. How the organization functions now can be compared with how it functioned at some time in the past;

2. How the organization functions now can be compared with how other organizations of the same type function;

3. How the organization functions now can be compared to how people within the organization would *like* it to function; or

4. How the organization functions now can be compared to how research and experience have demonstrated it *should* function.

To make the comparisons described in items 1 and 2, one must have answers to the same questions, summarized in a similar way, for either the same organization at more than one point in time or for more than one organization. In order to make the comparisons described in items 3 and 4, one needs an estimate of what people want and how they think their organizations should function, as well as the accumulated knowledge about effective functioning.

Survey-guided development relies upon a *standardized questionnaire* to gather the needed information for assessing how well an organization functions. In other words, a survey with a standard set of questions, shown to be relevant and meaningful in many types of organizations, is administered to organization members involved in the survey-guided development effort. With this information, one can make comparisons 1 and 2. The responses are stored and can be recalled when an organization wants to compare its present with its past functioning. An organization can also compare itself with all or certain kinds of other organizations that have used the survey. Comparisons such as those described in items 3 and 4 may be made by including relevant questions on the survey or by some more informal method, such as having people meet and list their preferences. These preferences and survey questions would then be compared with how the organization is functioning now, as described by responses to the standardized questions.

But are the questions being asked about the important aspects of organizational functioning? This is a central question. If the survey does not measure the important aspects, then it cannot identify the important problems. The answer, however, is quite straightforward. Aspects of organizational functioning are important when they:

1. Affect the performance, motivation, and reactions of organization members;

2. Fit into a coherent scheme or model of how successful organizations function; and

3. Are generally known to be crucial to the day-to-day or future survival of the organization.

The questions that are utilized on the questionnaire have been found to meet all three of the points listed. Furthermore, only reliable questions (i.e., those measuring stable characteristics not subject to meaningless variation) are included in the standard survey.

GOALS OF SURVEY-GUIDED DEVELOPMENT: THE MODEL OF EFFECTIVE ORGANIZATIONAL FUNCTIONING

Thus far, the discussion has focused on a general definition of survey-guided development and some description of the theory and assumptions underlying this approach. Attention now turns to the more specific kinds of things that survey-guided development is designed to accomplish.

The ultimate goal of survey-guided development is to facilitate interventions or changes in organizational functioning that will lead to increased organizational effectiveness by providing accurate and useful information about how an organization actually functions, how it might ideally function, and how to make the actual functioning more like the ideal functioning. As the previous sentence demonstrates, the ultimate goal of survey-guided development can be expressed by one statement. However, there are a number of requirements that need to be met if this goal is to be successfully accomplished.

First, the organization leaders and members involved in the development effort must have accurate and useful information about how effective organizations function or operate.

Second, the organization leaders must decide how their organization should ideally function.

Third, organization leaders and members must have accurate and useful information about how their organization functions currently and why it functions the way it does.

Fourth, organization leaders and members must be aware of discrepancies existing between current organizational functioning and how they would like their organization to function.

Fifth, where such discrepancies exist, organization leaders and members must try to lessen or eliminate them by planning and carrying out a sequence of activities designed to make the organization function more like their ideal model.

Sixth, after a certain period of time, the organization leaders and members must have information about the effects of the sequence of activities conducted to lessen the discrepancies.

Most people have some ideas about what makes an organization successful. They may not have intentionally developed these ideas nor mentioned them to anyone, but if asked "What makes an organization successful?" most people would respond fairly quickly. When they are put together in a coherent, meaningful way, these ideas can become a model of effective organizational functioning. When such a model has been tested and found to hold true, it can be said to be a valid (i.e., accurate and useful) model.

The following example may help to clarify what it means to have a valid model. Although Alfred thinks that the most effective organizations are run by autocratic leaders, his colleague, Sharon, believes that participative leaders are more effective. If Alfred and Sharon studied two organizations similar in all ways except for the type of leaders employed, and they found one organization to be more effective than

the other, the two models of effective leadership would have under-
gone an initial test. The model of leadership employed by the more
effective organization could be considered the more valid model of the
two. Although models of effective organizational functioning include
many factors in addition to leadership, this example illustrates one way
in which the validity of models is tested.

Survey-guided development is based on a model of effective functioning that has been tested in many kinds of organizations, and the
more like the model an organization functions, the more effective it
tends to be. Organization leaders and members embarking on a
survey-guided development effort must understand the model.

Once the ways in which the most effective organizations function is
known, the organization should decide how closely it wants to or can
approximate this model; that is, a goal should be set. In development
efforts it is important that organization leaders and members have a
model of effective functioning toward which they can strive, since
without such a model they would resemble nomads. Think of it this
way: When you don't know where you want to go, how do you find the
way, and how do you know when you've arrived?

Once a goal has been selected, information about how the organization functions can be collected and compared to how it would function
if the goal were achieved. If there is true commitment to the goal,
organization leaders and members are motivated to lessen the differences by planning changes and activities that will move the organization closer to the goal. After the changes have had a chance to work,
organizational functioning is assessed again to see how much movement actually took place. If there are still discrepancies, or if a new or
higher goal is set, additional changes are planned, implemented, and
evaluated. It is in this planned, monitored, and controlled manner that
the most constructive and lasting improvement occurs.

Feedback of survey data is one of the steps involved in accomplishing the ultimate goal of survey-guided development. The feedback
process may be carried out at two levels.

1. *Individual work-group level:* work-group data are summarized responses of individuals reporting to the same supervisor. These data
   are fed back at the individual work group level to those who
   supplied it.

2. *System Level:* combined responses of all organization members
   provide data describing the organization as a whole, which is fed
   back to the organization's leaders.

With feedback at both levels, change activities that are particularly relevant to individual groups or to the whole system can be planned and implemented by the individuals who are directly involved.

The feedback process, in addition to the other steps involved in survey-guided development, will be described in greater detail in later modules. At this point, it is important to gain a perspective of the sequence of steps involved in the development effort. The steps designed to accomplish the goal and meet the six requirements previously discussed are summarized in Figure 1.

THE CONSULTANT'S ROLE IN SURVEY-GUIDED DEVELOPMENT

What part can the consultant play in accomplishing the ultimate goal and meeting the requirements of the survey-guided development effort? *The primary role of the consultant is to act as a transducer—an energy link between accurate and useful scientific information regarding organizational functioning and change processes on the one hand, and the people involved in the development effort on the other.*

Technically, a transducer is a device that is set in motion by energy or power from one system and supplies energy or power in any other form to a second system. A telephone receiver is one example of such a device: It is activated by electric power and supplies acoustic or sound power to the surrounding air. In a similar way, the consultant acts like a transducer between sources of scientific information and particular organization units utilizing survey-guided development.

The notion of the consultant being a transducer is central. First, the consultant must take valid scientific information and make it understandable, relevant, and useful to those involved in the development effort. This means that the consultant takes in information from an external source and then gives the information, perhaps in a different form, to groups of people who are, again, external to himself.

In most cases, the source of scientific information will be researchers, and the receivers will be the particular people who are utilizing the survey-guided development approach. Figure 2 illustrates this aspect of the relationship between the consultant and these external units.

On the other hand, those involved in the development effort—the same people who receive the scientific information—generate information describing their particular work situation, which the consultant then adds to the source of valid information to be stored and available for future reference. This descriptive information can then be used to expand and modify the existing theory and activities associated with survey-guided development. Figure 3 illustrates this part of the consultant's role.

REQUIREMENTS	**STEPS**
1. Knowing a valid model of effective organizational functioning	1. Conceptual training (i.e., providing the model of effective organizational functioning)
2. Selecting an ideal state of organizational functioning	2. Goal setting
3. Collecting information about how the organization functions presently	3. Administration of the standardized survey to organization members
4. Recognizing discrepancies between actual and ideal functioning.	4. Diagnosis of present organizational functioning
5. Lessening discrepancies between actual and ideal functioning	5a. Feedback of survey data to the work groups that generated the data (i.e., feedback of work-group-level data), Planning and implementing action steps at the work-group level
	5b. Feedback of survey data about the whole organization to system leaders; planning and implementing action steps at the system level
6. Evaluating the effects of the change activities	6. Re-administration of standardized survey

Figure 1. Requirements of survey-guided development and the steps designed to meet them

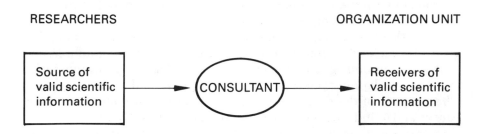

Figure 2. The first relationship between the consultant and external units

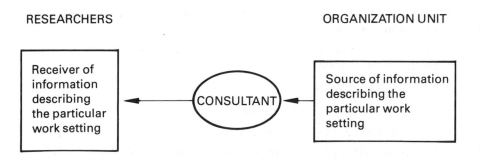

Figure 3. The second relationship between the consultant and external units

By fulfilling these two aspects of his transducer role, the consultant becomes an important link between the source of scientific information on the one hand, and the particular organization units he is involved with on the other. Figure 4 illustrates both aspects of the transducer role, including the notion that the transducing process occurs over and over again with the new information being integrated and utilized by both researchers and organization units.

Now that the consultant's transducer role has been described, the issue of what kinds of information are transduced should be addressed.

Survey-guided development may be viewed as including two separate but overlapping phases: a diagnostic phase and a change phase. The purpose of the diagnostic phase is to define problems and their causes and to indicate what changes are needed to solve the problems. The purpose of the change phase is to make the necessary corrections. The consultant needs a thorough understanding of several kinds of information that are important to each of the two phases. Furthermore, the consultant must have the necessary skills for transmitting information in a way that motivates and enables organization members to use it effectively.

During the diagnostic phase the kinds of information to be transduced include:

From the source of scientific information:

- The goals and requirements of survey-guided development;
- The activities through which the goals and requirements are accomplished;
- The ideal model of organizational functioning;
- The source of the questionnaire data (that is, who completed the questionnaire) and how the data were summarized;
- Ways in which the data are effective in creating a motivation to solve the problems identified.

From the people involved in the development effort:

- The specific ways in which problems are manifested;
- The specific causes of the problems;
- Which problems are inside or outside the control of the particular organization unit.

The people involved in the development effort also provide information crucial to the diagnosis, i.e., perceptions of how their organization functions as reported in the survey. Although not always the interpreter of this information, the consultant must learn to use it to facilitate the definition and solution of problems.

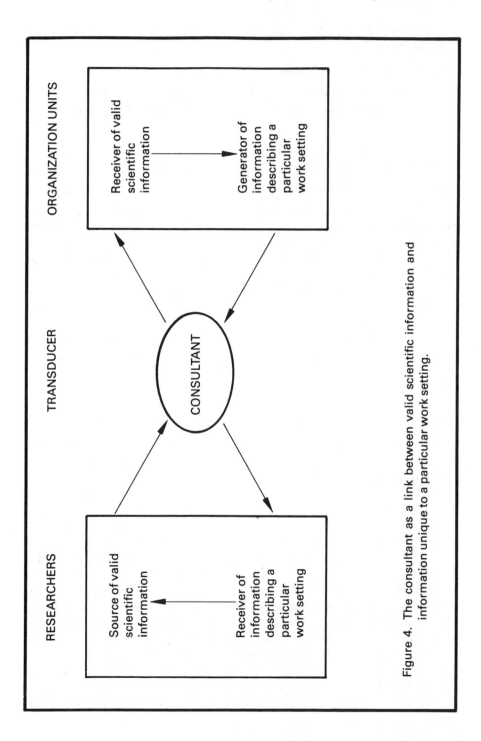

Figure 4. The consultant as a link between valid scientific information and information unique to a particular work setting.

During the change phase, the kinds of information transduced include:

From the source of scientific information:

- The change methods effective for solving a given problem;
- The people, materials, training, etc., needed to utilize the change methods.

From the people involved in the development effort:

- Their personal needs for information, skills, etc., necessary to make the change method work.

Information that the consultant gets from the source of scientific information provides a basis from which the development effort can start, since it provides evidence of what has been discovered and utilized in the past in many different settings and situations. On the other hand, the information the consultant gets from the people involved in the development effort provides a basis for the continuous updating and enlargement of the body of scientific information to be used in the future.

The consultant's role is a complex and crucial one in survey-guided development. Not only must the consultant master a vast amount of information, but he also needs particular skills for utilizing the information.

STRATEGY ISSUES IN SURVEY-GUIDED DEVELOPMENT

Because of the nature of survey-guided development, there are some general guidelines and perspectives that may affect the overall success of the development effort.

Basic to the development process is the theory that the motivation to change is created by the realization that the present state of organizational functioning differs from the ideal model, (i.e., a discrepancy exists between what is desired and what actually exists). However, it does not necessarily follow that the largest discrepancies create the greatest motivation to change. Rather, a moderate discrepancy may be most motivating. A moderate discrepancy often indicates a problem area that needs a significant amount of work but is not such a sizeable problem that it could not be solved within a reasonable time period and with available or obtainable resources. In contrast, very small discrepancies are easy to forget about, and huge discrepancies are discouraging. It is the consultant's job to point out and focus on motivating discrepancies.

In a development effort it is crucial that people near the top of the organization are motivated to change and are supportive of changes taking place lower in the organizational hierarchy. The importance of this motivation and support lies in the necessity for creating a climate of constructive change at the top levels, which will foster development at all levels below. Deciding how high in the organization one must go depends on the level at which people have some real power and control over what happens below them in the organization.

One way of building a climate that is supportive of change at the higher levels is to begin the development activities at those levels, and then soon after that beginning, start the activities at lower levels. This strategy has been found to be more effective than starting at the lowest levels of the organization, starting at all levels simultaneously, or dwelling exclusively on any one level.

In addition, it is useful to know why the organization unit became involved in the development effort in the first place. Was the development effort "laid on"; that is, were people told to use survey-guided development whether or not they wanted to? Was it just one more attempt to be innovative? Was it asked for because people felt a need to examine and solve problems? The answers to these questions and others like them indicate how much time and effort need to be put into establishing what survey-guided development has to offer the particular organization and how likely such an effort is to succeed. If the development effort has been forced on people, they may resist it, at least at first, regardless of how much sense the approach makes to them. A fair amount of time and effort might be needed to lessen this resistance. If the organization is trying survey-guided development merely to do something new and different, people may not be truly committed to changing the way they work, even when such changes would lead to constructive improvement. On the other hand, an organization that seeks survey-guided development because it wants assistance in identifying and solving problems is likely to respond quickly and constructively to the information and assistance it receives.

Finally, a few words about what survey-guided development is not:

- It is not a "shoot-from-the-hip" operation to be handled in a slipshod manner. Rather, it is a *systematic* program of activities that should be planned in advance.

- It is not a piecemeal operation from which bits and pieces get chosen or left out. Rather, it is a *coherent, integrated set* of activities designed to move the organization closer and closer to its desired level of functioning.

- It is rarely a "one-shot deal," rather, it involves *repeated cycles* of goal setting, diagnosis, treatment, and evaluation. Each cycle of activities should be designed to move the organization closer to its desired state. Each cycle should take into account changing conditions and, perhaps, changing goals.

ADAPTING SURVEY-GUIDED DEVELOPMENT TO SITUATIONAL CONSTRAINTS

The major purpose of this module has been to provide an overview of how survey-guided development should ideally progress. In some situations, however, constraints of time and resources preclude a full survey-guided development effort being conducted according to all the guidelines suggested in this manual. In cases where the ideal process cannot be carried out, the prescribed activities should be adapted to fit the situational constraints.

In approaching such an adaptation, certain minimum components of survey-guided development must be kept in mind. They are:

- Model-setting and goal-setting activities;
- Collection of data using a standardized, valid, and reliable survey;
- Organization and analysis of the survey data;
- Feedback of survey data;
- Problem identification;
- Solution generation and implementation; and
- Monitoring of effects of solutions.

Obviously, these are rather general terms and many of them could take various forms. Some forms require more time and resource investment than others.

One route to meeting time and resource constraints is to streamline the development effort by making use of self-training packages whenever possible. In fact, this manual is the result of efforts to reduce the amount of time needed for formal, face-to-face training of consultants. Another manual (Franklin, Hausser, & Spencer, 1977) has also been prepared specifically for model-setting activities.

In a similar vein, organization of survey data might be handled in a fairly standardized fashion. For example, a standard data-feedback package containing brief descriptions of the survey items and underlying concepts, as well as suggestions for how to summarize and display survey data, might be provided to each supervisor or manager receiving survey results. Such a package often reduces the time a consultant has to spend explaining technical details to individuals.

Another route is to create additional time and resources by developing resource people within the organizational unit involved in the effort. This approach serves two functions. First, it reduces the amount of time required of outside consultants and previously trained in-house consultants. Second, it increases the number of organization members who really understand what survey-guided development involves by providing some number of them with relevant information and skills.

All of the above suggestions involve adapting survey-guided development to situational constraints by increasing efficiency while still maintaining all the prescribed development activities. In some situations, however, it may become necessary to reduce the scope of the effort. It has already been stated that, ideally, survey-guided development activities focus on development at two levels: the system level and the group level. If time and resource constraints do not allow for such a complete development effort, system-level development should take priority over development activities at the work-group level.

In strategizing any such adaptation of survey-guided development, it is recommended that in each situation the effort be planned with an ideal set of activities in mind. Where real-world conditions impinge on this ideal, adaptation and compromise are necessary. However, taking this approach results in an effort that more closely approximates the ideal than one that was developed by first identifying all possible constraints in a situation and their potential impact and then trying to design activities that will not conflict with them. In other words, be constrained only when you are forced to be.

Module 2
Using a Standardized Questionnaire: The Survey of Organizations

This module covers (1) features of a standardized survey and why it is chosen as a tool for gathering data in survey-guided development, (2) the structure and content of the Survey of Organizations, which will be referred to throughout subsequent modules in this manual, and (3) essential aspects of the consultant's role in preparing for survey administration to organization members through his initial meetings with the designated organizational project leader. The information provided in this module enables the consultant to answer questions from organization members regarding the importance and usefulness of the survey and the data it generates.

WHAT IS A STANDARDIZED SURVEY?

Survey-guided development is based on perceptions of organizational functioning gathered from organization members who respond to a standardized questionnaire. To understand why the survey is an essential tool used throughout the process, the characteristics of a standardized survey must first be considered. Primarily, the term standardized refers to the fact that the survey is comprised of predetermined questions and answer alternatives, uniformly arranged, explained, and administered to all respondents. The questionnaire is devised so that its content is relevant to a large population of people who will use it, and also so that it may be used over a considerable period of time without major revision. When these conditions are met, the same survey can be administered to many groups of people over time. This possibility of gathering data from large numbers of people allows all responses to be grouped together to form norms for the survey, which add to its standardized nature. Briefly, norms are aver- aged survey responses over large numbers of respondents, which can be used as a standard with which subsequent respondent groups can compare their data. Norms are more fully discussed in Section 3 of this module, but they are mentioned here as an important part of the useful- ness of a standardized survey.

The third important characteristic of a standardized survey, particu- larly one for use in survey-guided development, is that it is closely tied to a theory of organizational functioning. The theory is crucial since it provides a basis for (1) deciding what questions should be included, (2) using the data to accurately describe the state of the organization at the time of the survey administration, and (3) interpreting responses and using the data to improve organizational functioning. The importance of the theory underlying the survey will become more clear in later modules that explore specific ways in which data are used at both the work-group and total-system levels.

WHY USE A STANDARDIZED SURVEY?

There are several reasons why a survey is the basis for collecting data for use in the development effort. First, a standardized survey can be efficiently scored and administered to many people. This is important because it allows us to gather multiple perceptions about organization and work-group functioning which are useful for assessment and feed- back activities in survey-guided development. The more individual perceptions are gathered, the more the data accurately describes as- pects of the work situation as they truly operate.

Second, since the survey is tied to a theory of organizational func- tioning, it measures behaviors and conditions that influence various outcome characteristics (e.g., turnover, efficiency, productivity). This allows us to look at aspects of the work situation that partially cause and influence the quality of these system outputs, rather than measuring only outputs themselves.

Third, survey data, ideally, are provided by all organization mem- bers. Consequently, the data provide tangible, manageable informa- tion that system members themselves can use as a tool for identifying the strengths and weaknesses of their unit or work group. The data encourage personnel to look at specific examples of concrete condi- tions and behaviors that can be improved. They can then plan, on the basis of what their data show, to work toward an increased level of effective functioning.

SOME CHARACTERISTICS OF AN EFFICIENT SURVEY

Survey Items

The single survey question is the most basic unit of data and provides the most specific information. This section focuses on considerations that should be made in deciding how items are to be included on the survey. In taking the intended respondents into account, each question should be clear and relevant to the respondent. Each question should be geared to some concrete aspect of the work situation, and should not be asking about more than one behavior or condition at a time. Answer alternatives should also be clearly relevant to the question and sufficient in number and content for the respondent to be able to express his opinion adequately. The survey should include an optimal number (neither too few nor too many) of questions to adequately measure the facets of any given area of the work situation. The ability of the question to measure what it is supposed to be measuring, as well as its relevance over time and slight variance in work situations, should be taken into account. In this regard, it is sometimes useful to include questions that have, from previous use, been shown to be effective in measuring particular areas of the work situation. Finally, any item chosen for inclusion on the survey should be justified in terms of its usefulness (1) for research, or to test whether a question is in fact useful in measuring an important aspect of the work situation, (2) for assessment of the present state of organizational functioning, or (3) in feeding back the data to respondents, and helping them recall specific instances in their work environment that are related to the area considered in the item.

Indices

An index is a unit of data formed by grouping several related survey items together and obtaining an average score over these items. The formation of indices make the survey more efficient because it is often difficult to measure a domain of organizational functioning with a single survey item. Several items may be needed to adequately measure the various facets of a larger or more general domain of functioning. In order to decide which items may profitably be included in a given index, it is helpful if the items have been shown by previous data collection and research to be related. However, when such evidence is not available, you can tentatively group items with related content to see whether they do relate on the basis of the data you are collecting. The main concern in grouping items to form indices is that the items should not be asking the same basic question, but neither should they be so unrelated that they do not measure facets of a common domain of functioning.

Norms

Once the survey has been administered to many people from several organizations, all the data can be summarized together to obtain survey norms. Basically, norms may be described as average scores from all respondents on all survey items and indices. These scores are used by smaller groups of respondents—say, a single organization or work group—as a standard against which their scores may be compared. When a smaller group compares its scores to those of the larger group, it gets an indication of how well it is doing relative to the norms. In order for this comparison to be meaningful, the standard group and the smaller group should have some characteristics in common: both groups should have similar organizational characteristics, such as hierarchical levels or general job types; and both groups should have provided survey data at reasonably close time points. Most important, the standard group should be large enough to represent feelings of all people who have not been surveyed. In other words, the more people and organizations that are included in the norms, the more the norms provide a realistic and representative indication of how all people in similar job situations feel about the aspects of their jobs measured by the survey.

The following sections of this module focus on the Survey of Organizations, the questionnaire used and developed by the Organization Development Research Program at the Institute for Social Research, University of Michigan. The extensive research involved in devising and refining the Survey of Organizations allows us to use it as a worthy example of the terms and concepts mentioned up to this point and of material to be introduced in subsequent modules.

THE SURVEY OF ORGANIZATIONS

The Survey of Organizations, presently in its fifth (1974) edition, is a standardized machine-scored questionnaire developed since 1966 to measure certain critical dimensions of organizational climate, supervisory leadership, peer behavior, group processes, job characteristics, motivation, and satisfaction. (For an extensive description of the history, item and index analysis, and use of the Survey of Organizations, see Taylor & Bowers, 1972.) The Survey is a measurement tool used to generate data that provide an organization with quantified information regarding its level of functioning. The data are used to help the organization focus on and deal with problems in the area of organizational development, so that it can move toward a more effective level of functioning.

The 1974 edition of the Survey contains 124 core questions printed with response codes that are processed and summarized by automated equipment. (Module 3 explains in greater detail the ways in which the data may be summarized.) Of these 124 items, the last five are demographic questions. These items may be used to see how various respondent characteristics influence answers on the core questions. To get this kind of information, data may be grouped by demographic categories during processing. The survey booklet also includes answer spaces for forty-two optional questions. These allow organization leaders to include questions of their own that are of particular relevance to the work situation in their organization. An additional feature of the Survey format is the identification-of-supervisor grid that directly precedes a series of questions regarding the behavior of the respondent's immediate supervisor. The five-digit code number assigned to each respondent's supervisor is to be provided in this grid. This information is used solely to enable the questionnaire to be meaningfully processed and summarized by work group, with all other surveys having the same supervisory number.

A more specific examination of the survey content and structure is undertaken on the following pages. This is done by providing a breakdown of the Survey items (except demographic) by index. A conceptual description of each index is provided along with survey items grouped together to measure the designated area of functioning. All survey items have an answer alternative scale from 1 to 5, where 1 indicates *least* and 5 the *most* effective degree of functioning, which in most cases corresponds to the following:

1: To a very little extent
2: To a little extent
3: To some extent
4: To a great extent
5: To a very great extent

Items representing exceptions to this response scale are noted. Also, several questions request respondents' "actual" and "ideal" ratings; that is, the respondent is asked the same question in terms of how the situation presently exists and then in terms of how he would ideally like the situation to be. As suggested in Module 1, this provides a built-in standard of comparison within the survey data by allowing organization members to examine discrepancies between their actual situations and their ideal goals to see where the greatest needs for change exist. Questions with actual and ideal components are concerned largely with specific aspects of supervisory and peer behaviors and characteristics of the respondent's job.

Following the breakdown of items by index, a listing is provided of the remaining items that are not included in an index. This listing includes references for ways in which these single items can provide supportive evidence when interpreting the data.

THE SURVEY OF ORGANIZATIONS QUESTIONNAIRE
DESCRIPTION OF INDICES AND COMPONENT ITEMS

(Index numbers refer to the sequential location of index scores on the computer printout sheets. See Module 3 for sample work group data and Module 6 for sample systemic data printouts. All items use the five-point extent scale unless otherwise noted.)

Organizational Climate

Organizational climate: refers to the organization-wide conditions, policies, and procedures within which each work group operates. These conditions and policies are created for a work group by other groups, especially by those above it in the organizational hierarchy. Climate conditions set bounds on what does and what can go on within any work group. Aspects of climate, as listed here, can help or hinder conditions within groups, or may do both at the same time.

CLIMATE INDICES

193. *Decision-Making Practices:* measures whether those who make decisions in various instances are appropriate; whether information needed by decision makers is accessible; and whether organization members affected by decisions are consulted before decisions are made.

Items:

31. How are objectives set in this organization?
    1. Objectives are announced with no opportunity to raise questions or give comments.
    2. Objectives are announced and explained, and an opportunity is then given to ask questions.
    3. Objectives are drawn up, but are discussed with subordinates and sometimes modified before being issued.
    4. Specific alternative objectives are drawn up by supervisors, and subordinates are asked to discuss them and indicate the one they think is best.
    5. Problems are presented to those persons who are involved, and the objectives felt to be best are then set by the

subordinates and the supervisor jointly, by group participation and discussion.

32. In this organization, to what extent are decisions made at those levels where the most adequate and accurate information is available?

33. When decisions are being made, to what extent are the persons affected asked for their ideas?

34. People at all levels of an organization usually have know-how that could be of use to decision-makers. To what extent is information widely shared in this organization so that those who make decisions have access to all available know-how?

191. *Communication Flow:* the extent to which the flow of information throughout the organization is facilitated upward, downward, and in lateral directions or channels.

Items:

12. How adequate for your work group is the information it gets about what is going on in other departments or shifts?

13. How receptive are people above your supervisor to ideas and suggestions from your work group?

14. To what extent does this organization tell your work group what it needs to know to do its job in the best possible way?

192. *Motivational Conditions:* measures several factors of organizational functioning that influence individual motivation on the job, including: the way disagreements across units are handled; the extent to which people are intrinsically or extrinsically motivated; and whether organizational conditions generally encourage hard work.

Items:

15. How are differences and disagreements between units or departments handled in this organization?

    1. Disagreements are almost always avoided, denied, or suppressed.

    2. Disagreements are often avoided, denied, or suppressed.

    3. Sometimes disagreements are accepted and worked through; sometimes they are avoided or suppressed.

    4. Disagreements are usually accepted as necessary and desirable and are worked through.

    5. Disagreements are almost always accepted as necessary and desirable and are worked through.

23. Why do people work hard in this organization?
    1. Just to keep their jobs and avoid being chewed out.
    2. To keep their jobs *and* to make money.
    3. To keep their jobs, make money, *and* to seek promotions.
    4. To keep their jobs, make money, seek promotions, *and* for the satisfaction of a job well done.
    5. To keep their jobs, make money, seek promotions, do a satisfying job, *and* because other people in their work group expect it.
25. To what extent are there things about working here (people, policies, or conditions) that encourage you to work hard?

190. *Human-Resources Primacy:* measures whether the organization values its people as worthwhile assets or resources by the way it organizes work activities, shows concern for employee welfare, and tries to improve working conditions.

Items:

8. To what extent does this organization have a real interest in the welfare and happiness of those who work here?
9. How much does this organization try to improve working conditions?
11. To what extent are work activities sensibly organized in this organization?

196. *Lower Level Influence:* describes the influence that lowest level supervisors and nonsupervisory personnel have on departmental matters.

Items:

In general, how much say or influence does each of the following groups of people have on what goes on *in your department?*

Answer alternatives

1. Little or no influence
2. Some
3. Quite a bit
4. A great deal
5. A very great deal of influence

27. Lowest level supervisors (foremen, office supervisors, etc.)
29. Employees (people who have no subordinates)

189. *Technological Readiness:* measures whether the organization is viewed as adequately maintaining and updating work methods and sufficient equipment for employees to do their jobs efficiently.

Items:

    7. To what extent is this organization generally quick to use improved work methods?

    99. To what extent are the equipment and resources you have to do your work with adequate, efficient, and well maintained?

Supervisory Leadership

Supervisory leadership: comprised of interpersonal and task-related behaviors that describe the way supervisors are viewed by their subordinates. The following indices measuring the behavior of supervisors include two-part items that describe present behavior ("how it is now") and ideal supervisory behavior ("how you would like it to be") for the same question stem. Although items and indices are worded and numbered for the actual rather than ideal functioning, index and item numbers for the ideal are provided.

SUPERVISORY-LEADERSHIP INDICES

173. *Support* (174. *Support—Ideal:* items 37, 39, 41): measures whether supervisor's behavior lets his subordinates know that they are worthwhile persons doing useful work.

Items:

    36. How friendly and easy to approach is your supervisor (now)?

    38. When you talk with your supervisor, to what extent does he pay attention to what you're saying (now)?

    40. To what extent is your supervisor willing to listen to your problems (now)?

179. *Team Building* (180. *Team Building—Ideal:* items 53, 55): measures whether supervisor's behavior encourages subordinates to develop close, cooperative working relationships with one another.

Items:

    52. To what extent does your supervisor encourage the persons who work for him to work as a team (now)?

    54. To what extent does your supervisor encourage people who work for him to exchange opinions and ideas (now)?

175. *Goal Emphasis* (176. *Goal Emphasis—Ideal:* items 43, 45): measures whether supervisor's behavior stimulates a contagious enthusiasm among his subordinates for doing a good job (*not* pressure).

Items:

42. How much does your supervisor encourage people to give their best effort (now)?

44. To what extent does your supervisor maintain high standards of performance (now)?

177. *Work Facilitation* (178. *Work Facilitation—Ideal:* items 47, 49, 51): measures whether supervisor's behavior removes roadblocks to doing a good job.

Items:

46. To what extent does your supervisor show you how to improve your performance (now)?

48. To what extent does your supervisor provide the help you need so that you can plan and schedule work ahead of time (now)?

50. To what extent does your supervisor offer new ideas for solving job-related problems (now)?

Supervisory-Needs Indices

Supervisory-needs indices: [1] *although these indices are not part of the four leadership indices, they do deal with subordinates' perceptions of their supervisors' behaviors and, therefore, are listed at this point. These indices measure whether supervisors are viewed as having adequate information, values, or skills to be effective managers. All supervisory needs items are prefaced by the following:*

In order to be an effective leader, a supervisor needs certain kinds of information, skills, values, and situations. To what extent does *your* supervisor have each of the following:

INDICES:

200. *Supervisor Needs Information*

60. Information about how his people see and feel about things?

61. Knowledge of what it takes to be a good leader?

---

[1]These indices were clustered in this form for the first time on the 1974 Survey of Organizations. Although there is good evidence to support their relatedness in this form, conclusive testing of their relationship has yet to be made as of this writing.

201. *Supervisor Needs Values*

> 62. An attitude which encourages participation and commitment from those who work for him?

> 66. Interest in and concern for the people who work for him?

202. *Supervisor Needs Skills*

> 63. Administrative skill?

> 64. Skills for getting along with others?

> (single, non-index, supervisory-needs item measuring adequacy of work situation:

> 65. A work situation which *allows* him to be a good leader?)

Peer Leadership

Peer leadership: comprised of interpersonal and task-related behaviors of work-group members toward each other. Peer behavior is measured by items similar to those measuring supervisory leadership and, therefore, include both actual and ideal components of the same question.

PEER-LEADERSHIP INDICES

181. *Support* (182. *Support—Ideal:* items 71, 73, 75): measures whether behavior of group members toward one another contributes to their mutual feeling of being worthwhile persons doing useful work.

Items:

> 70. How friendly and easy to approach are the persons in your work group (now)?

> 72. When you talk with persons in your work group, to what extent do they pay attention to what you're saying (now)?

> 74. To what extent are persons in your work group willing to listen to your problems (now)?

187. *Team Building* (188. *Team Building—Ideal:* items 87, 89, 91): measures whether behavior of group members toward one another encourages the development of close, cooperative working relationships.

Items:

> 86. How much do persons in your work group encourage each other to work as a team (now)?

88. How much do persons in your work group emphasize a *team* goal (now)?

90. To what extent do persons in your work group exchange opinions and ideas (now)?

183. *Goal Emphasis* (184. *Goal Emphasis—Ideal:* items 77, 79): measures whether behavior of group members toward one another stimulates a mutually contagious enthusiasm for doing a good job.

Items:

76. How much do persons in your work group encourage each other to give their best effort (now)?

78. To what extent do persons in your work group maintain high standards of performance (now)?

185. *Work Facilitation* (186. *Work Facilitation—Ideal:* items 81, 83, 85): measures whether behavior of group members is mutually helpful; whether group members help one another remove roadblocks to doing a good job.

Items:

80. To what extent do persons in your work group help you find ways to do a better job (now)?

82. To what extent do persons in your work group provide the help you need so that you can plan, organize, and schedule work ahead of time (now)?

84. To what extent do persons in your work group offer each other new ideas for solving job-related problems (now)?

195. *Group-Process Index:* measures those things that characterize the group as a team and whether group members work together well or poorly. The way in which group members share information, make decisions, and solve problems determines the group's effectiveness and the quality of its outputs.

Items:

92. To what extent does your work group plan together and coordinate its efforts?

93. To what extent does your work group make good decisions and solve problems well?

94. To what extent do persons in your work group know what their jobs are and how to do them well?

95. To what extent is information about important events and situations shared within your work group?

96. To what extent does your work group really want to meet its objectives successfully?

97. To what extent is your work group able to respond to unusual work demands placed on it?

98. To what extent do you have confidence and trust in the persons in your work group?

---

197. *Job-Challenge Index* (198. *Job Challenge—Ideal:* items 118, 119, 120): measures whether actual (and ideal) job characteristics include challenging features, such as opportunity for learning new things, for getting ahead, and for using those skills in which employees are most proficient.

Preface to items: To what extent does each of the following statements describe *the job you have now?*

Items:

112. I can *learn* new things, learn new skills.

113. It provides good chances for getting ahead.

114. It *uses* my skills and abilities—lets me do the things I can do best.

203. *Experienced-Bureaucracy Index:* measures whether the individual experiences unreasonable roadblocks or constraints when trying to get things done or to get help on the job.

Items (preceded by preface for items 112-114):

115. I don't get endlessly referred from person to person when I need help.

116. I don't have to go through a lot of "red tape" to get things done.

117. I don't get hemmed in by longstanding rules and regulations that no one seems to be able to explain.

204. *Aversion-to-Bureaucracy Index:* measures whether the individual would be averse to bureaucratic practices and procedures in an ideal job situation; this index is actually the "ideal" form of Index 203, Experienced Bureaucracy.

Preface to items: In thinking about the kind of job you *would like to have* (whether or not you have it now), to what extent is each of the following important to you?

Items:

    121. A job where I don't get endlessly referred from person to person when I need help.

    122. A job where I don't have to go through a lot of "red tape" to get things done.

    123. A job where I am not hemmed in by longstanding rules and regulations that no one seems to be able to explain.

199. *Goal-Integration Index:* measures whether the needs of the organization and the needs of individual organization members are compatible and are both being fulfilled.

Items:

    124. To what extent is the organization you work for effective in getting you to meet its needs and contribute to its effectiveness?

    125. To what extent does the organization you work for do a good job of meeting your needs as an individual?

194. *Satisfaction Index:* measures whether organization members are satisfied with economic and related rewards, adequacy of immediate supervisor, effectiveness of the organization as a system, the job as a whole, compatibility with fellow work group members, and present and future progress within the organization. This index is a measure of output, reflecting the extent to which the foregoing measured areas function effectively.

Items:

    16. All in all, how satisfied are you with the persons in your work group?

    17. All in all, how satisfied are you with your supervisor?

    18. All in all, how satisfied are you with your job?

    19. All in all, how satisfied are you with this organization?

    20. Considering your skills and the effort you put into the work, how satisfied are you with your pay?

    21. How satisfied do you feel with the progress you have made *up to now*?

    22. How satisfied do you feel with your chances for getting ahead in this organization *in the future*?

Survey-of-Organizations Summary Sheet
Indices and Component-Item Numbers

Organizational Climate

    Decision-Making Practices: 31, 32, 33, 34
    Communication Flow: 12, 13, 14
    Motivational Conditions: 15, 23, 25
    Human-Resources Primacy: 8, 9, 11
    Lower Level Influence: 27, 29
    Technological Readiness: 7, 99

Supervisory Leadership

    Support (Actual): 36, 38, 40
    Support (Ideal): 37, 39, 41
    Team Building (Actual): 52, 54
    Team Building (Ideal): 53, 55
    Goal Emphasis (Actual): 42, 44
    Goal Emphasis (Ideal): 43, 45
    Work Facilitation (Actual): 46, 48, 50
    Work Facilitation (Ideal): 47, 49, 51

Supervisory-Needs Indices

    Supervisor Needs Information: 60, 61
    Supervisor Needs Values: 62, 66
    Supervisor Needs Skills: 63, 64

Peer Leadership

    Support (Actual): 70, 72, 74
    Support (Ideal): 71, 73, 75
    Team Building (Actual): 86, 88, 91
    Team Building (Ideal): 87, 89, 91
    Goal Emphasis (Actual): 76, 78
    Goal Emphasis (Ideal): 77, 79
    Work Facilitation (Actual): 80, 82, 84
    Work Facilitation (Ideal): 81, 83, 85

Group-Process Index: 92, 93, 94, 95, 96, 97, 98

Job Challenge (Actual): 112, 113, 114

Job Challenge (Ideal): 118, 119, 120

Experienced Bureaucracy: 115, 116, 117

Aversion to Bureaucracy: 121, 122, 123

Goal Integration: 124, 125

Satisfaction: 16, 17, 18, 19, 20, 21, 22

Single Survey of Organizations Items
(Survey Items Not Clustered into an Index)

These items are listed with alternative indices or larger areas with which their scores can be compared to get supporting evidence for suggested strong or weak index areas. As suggested in later modules, when interpreting data for a work group or organization, you should focus on major features and not necessarily make use of every survey item included in the data. It *is* important to be sure that you consider all the data in deciding where to focus.

10. *To what extent does this organization have clear-cut reasonable goals and objectives?*
    Compare:
    - Item 19 (Satisfaction Index): satisfaction with the organization
    - Climate indices: Human-Resources Primacy, Communication Flow

24. *To what extent do you enjoy performing the actual day-to-day activities that make up your job?*
    Compare:
    - Item 18 (Satisfaction Index): satisfaction with the job
    - Actual Job Characteristics items 108-111
    - Job-Challenge (Actual) Index

26. *In general, how much say or influence do you have on what goes on in your work group?*
    Compare:
    - Items 67-69: relating to the way supervisor handles decision making involving work group
    - Peer-Support (Actual) Index
    - Item 98 (Group-Process Index): confidence and trust in work group members

28. *Influence of top managers on departmental matters*

30. *Influence of middle managers on departmental matters*
    Compare:
    - Lower-Level-Influence Index:
        27. Influence of first-line supervisors on departmental matters
        29. Influence of nonsupervisory employees on departmental matters
    - Decision-Making Practices, Communication-Flow indices

35. *To what extent do different units or departments plan together and coordinate their efforts?*
    Compare:
    - Item 12 (Communication-Flow Index): lateral communication
    - Item 15 (Motivational-Conditions Index): differences between departments worked through
    - Item 59: supervisor represents your work group to other units

56. *To what extent do you feel your supervisor has confidence and trust in you?*

57. *To what extent do you have confidence and trust in your supervisor?*
    Compare:
    - Supervisory-Support (Actual) Index
    - Discrepancies between scores on Supervisory-Support Actual and Supervisory-Support Ideal indices
    - Items 67-69: relating to the way the supervisor handles decision making involving work group
    - Item 59: supervisor represents your work group to other units

58. *To what extent does your supervisor handle well the technical side of his job—for example, general expertness, knowledge of job, technical skills needed in his profession or trade?*
    Compare:
    - Supervisor-Needs-Skills Index

59. *To what extent does your supervisor do a good job of representing your work group to other units? ("Represent" means telling others about what your work group has done and can do, as well as explaining the problems facing it and its readiness to do things.)*
    Compare:
    - Item 13 (Communication-Flow Index): upward communication
    - Item 57: you have confidence and trust in your supervisor
    - Item 35: departments plan and coordinate

65. *(To what extent does your supervisor have) A work situation which allows him to be a good leader?*
    This single item is part of the Supervisory-Needs group, see the previous explanation of Supervisory-Needs Indices.

Preface to items 67, 68, 69: when it is necessary for decisions to be made that affect your work group, to what extent does your supervisor do each of the following *before* final decisions are made?

67. *Provide the members of your work group with information about the decisions.*

68. *Ask for opinions and ideas from members of your work group.*

69. *Meet with his subordinates as a group, present problems that must be solved, and work with the group to find solutions.*
    Compare:
    - Supervisory Team-Building (Actual) Index
    - Items 56, 57 (see above): mutual confidence and trust between supervisor and subordinates
    - Item 26: influence on what goes on in work group

Items 100-107: Job-Motivation items, covering rewards from doing job well; others' expectations, and demands from individual in doing his job.

100. *When it comes to doing your job well, to what extent does trying hard make any difference?*

101. *To what extent does doing your job well lead to things like pay increases, bonuses, and promotions?*

102. *To what extent does doing your job well give you a feeling of personal satisfaction?*

103. *To what extent does doing your job well lead to things like recognition and respect from those you work with?*

104. *To what extent does doing your job well lead to things like disapproval and rejection from those you work with?*

105. *To what extent are you clear about what people expect you to do on your job?*

106. *To what extent are there times on your job when one person wants you to do one thing and someone else wants you to do something different?*

107. *To what extent do people expect too much from you on your job?*
    Compare:
    - Motivational-Conditions Index
    - Supervisory-Goal Emphasis (Actual)

- Peer-Goal Emphasis (Actual)
- Satisfaction item 18: satisfaction with the job
- Item 108: my job gives me the chance to find out how well I am doing

Items 108-111: characteristics of present job.

Preface: to what extent does each of the following statements describe the job you have now?

108. *It gives me the opportunity to find out how well I am doing*

109. *It lets me do a number of different things*

110. *It gives me the freedom to do pretty much what I want*

111. *It lets me do a whole piece of work (as opposed to doing part of a job which is finished by someone else).*
    Compare:
- Item 18: Satisfaction with job
- Items 100-104: various consequences of doing the job well
- Job-Challenge (Actual) Index

PREPARATION FOR SURVEY ADMINISTRATION

A very important part of the consultant's role is his initial meetings with internal project coordinators and his presentation of the purpose and sequence of the survey-guided development effort. It is important that system leaders be well informed about the effort and invested in it from the beginning, since their help and support is a key to the success of the process. Therefore, a comprehensive and organized approach on your part should enhance subsequent interaction, while a disorganized presentation may lower credibility and hinder future acceptance of the program by organization members.

Part of your initial discussions focus around the survey and the process of administering it to organization members. You must make sure, first, that personnel in charge of the development effort know and support the purpose of using the survey, and are aware of how the data will and should be used. It should be stressed that survey results are to be used to assist organization members in assessing their system and work-group functioning; the data are only for the constructive use of the units surveyed and will not be used for evaluative purposes at higher levels. Modules 3 and 6 describe guidelines for establishing, before the administration of the survey, and then maintaining a policy on confidentiality of both work-group and systemic data. The focus in this section is on preparing all personnel for the survey administration.

It is important that you arrange for all personnel to be notified of the survey administration. Indicate to those involved in this task the value of including in this notification something about the purpose of the survey and how the data that is provided by the organization members will be used. You must also arrange schedules for administration of the survey and for facilities where sessions can take place, and notify respondents accordingly. These arrangements should be made with someone who is knowledgeable about the work and shift schedules, the availability of personnel and facilities, and who has the authority to arrange schedules. Be sure that adequate time (a total of approximately one and one-half to two hours) and space are provided at each administration session. An area is needed that allows all participants to be seated with a writing surface available, and where noise and disruptions are minimized.

Part of the preparation includes briefing those people who, in addition to yourself, will be involved in administering the survey and providing instructions to respondents. The manner in which the survey is presented to respondents may have a greater influence on the respondents' attitudes than often is realized. By setting the atmosphere and helping to alleviate the respondents' reservations about filling out the survey, the people who administer the survey act as cues to the kinds of responses that are provided. Respondents should feel free to ask questions to clarify aspects of the procedure they may not understand.

The instructions should include definitions of terms used in the survey so that all respondents have the same notion of what information the survey questions are asking for. Such terms would include work group, supervisor, organization, and the like. It is also important that unusual aspects of the procedure be explained in a step-by-step manner, for example, how to fill out the Supervisory Identification Grid, or where to answer optional questions, if they are used. The administrator should tell respondents what will be done with the completed surveys. Individuals who are reporting their feelings about their peers, supervisors, and jobs are entitled to know what will be done with the information they provide. In this connection, respondent confidentiality should be emphasized. It should be mentioned that the information will be used to help improve work conditions and organization effectiveness. When respondents feel confident that their privacy will not be violated and their responses are an essential contribution to a worthwhile effort, they are more likely to take the survey seriously and to report their true perceptions.

The order and delivery of instructions should be presented as uniformly as possible from session to session in order to avoid biasing responses by the way the survey is presented. Minor modifications may be necessary for specific respondent groups, but the same information should be provided to all respondents. Therefore, it is essential that before the administration sessions, people who administer the survey consider together the content and order of instructions and the possible questions or apprehensions that respondents might have. Survey administrators create a more relaxed atmosphere if they themselves are comfortable with the instruction procedure and purpose of the survey. During preparatory meetings, administrators can outline a uniform sequence of instructions. Role playing the delivery of instructions helps to solidify their order and aspects that should be emphasized.

During survey sessions, sealed boxes should be provided, both for the depositing of completed surveys and for visibly reinforcing the fact that individual surveys will not be viewed by anyone. Respondents should know that the data will be processed and statistically summarized before any score reports of the data are returned to the organization. If possible, to save time and confusion, all necessary equipment (pencils, surveys, boxes) for the session should be gathered and set out before the respondents arrive.

Finally, when administering the survey it is important not to take anything for granted. Although the administrator may be familiar with the survey and convinced of its importance, he must provide explicit instructions and explanations for respondents. As a consultant, your role is to be sure that those who administer the survey are aware of the importance of their task. The data you will be working with throughout the survey-guided development effort will be only as good as the accuracy and frankness of the survey responses provided by organization members during this initial phase of the process.

Section II

Activities and Concepts at the Work-Group Level

Overview of Group-Level Development

This section focuses on the work group as the fundamental component of any organization. It deals with how to understand, organize, and present survey data, and how to involve a work group in identifying and solving its problems. Data analysis, discussion, and problem-solving activities at the work-group level are described in detail.

In many of these activities, the consultant acts mainly as an observer and facilitator, intervening with information or process skills only when that becomes necessary for the continued progress of the meeting. Because of this relatively passive stance, it is important that the work-group supervisor be committed to the work-group feedback meeting and adequately prepared for it.

When time and resource constraints do not allow complete feedback of group-level data, an effort should be made to, at least, feed back group-level data to the top-level group or groups. The leaders attending these sessions may be able to learn enough about the kinds of activities that should occur to conduct feedback meetings with their own work group. A valuable tool for these work-group supervisors would be some standardized set of explanatory material that could be used to analyze and discuss their data. Such a tool might be called a group-data feedback package and is described in Module 3. Another alternative might enable work-group feedback sessions to be conducted: the consultant could train additional people within the organization in the interpretation of data and in the activities and skills needed for group-feedback and problem-solving sessions. These internal resource people would then be responsible for guiding group-level development activities.

One note about the format of this manual. Key phrases, e.g., [source of the data], are used to list examples of interventions the consultant might utilize in various situations. The interventions are described in Module 9 and may be referred to by their key phrases. If you are not already familiar with how to locate these descriptions, read the introduction to Module 9 before proceeding with this section.

Module 3
Understanding Work-Group Data
and Preparing Data Displays

This module covers the basic skills and strategies you will need to organize and interpret group-level data. It begins by examining what work-group data are, and goes on from there to explain the format in which you will receive the data. The remaining sections cover content areas that will help you understand what the data mean, and how to prepare the data for the group's supervisor. Suggestions are made for displaying the data in order to highlight the major features to be discussed in the work group feedback meeting.

WHAT ARE WORK-GROUP DATA?

Once the survey has been administered to organization members, all the survey information must be organized in a useful manner. The first step in organizing the data takes place as the surveys are processed by computer. During processing, the data are summarized in a variety of ways. Responses are grouped together and averaged (1) across the whole organization, (2) by functional or departmental areas, (3) by hierarchical level within the organization, and (4) by work group. Of these four ways of summarizing the data, the first three—by total organization, by functional area, and by hierarchical level—are termed systemic data because they average responses of people throughout the whole organization. The function of systemic data in assessing the organization's functioning is discussed in later modules. (See Modules 6 and 7.) The fourth way of organizing the data, by individual work group, is the focus of this module.

It was mentioned in Module 2 that the term *work group* must be clearly defined when the survey is administered. This is important because several of the survey questions pertain to the respondent's work group, and respondents must have their work-group members in mind when answering these questions. A work group is defined as all individuals who report to the same supervisor. Work-group members may have different tasks, different salary levels, or may not actually work together in doing their jobs. The important thing is that they all report directly to the same supervisor. The clarity of this term is also important for another reason. Work-group members' responses are grouped by assigning the same supervisor identification code to all members of a work group. During computer processing, the responses of all people with the same identification code are combined. When the data are returned to the organization, the work group is the smallest unit of data reported. Data summarized at the work-group level serve two purposes. First, individual anonymity is maintained because only the average of work-group members' responses is reported. Second, work-group data provide multiple perceptions of how the work group functions. This is important because multiple perceptions are usually more accurate than the perceptions of one or a few people. (In fact, if fewer than three people from any work group fill out the survey, data for that work group are not returned to the organization. Reporting data from only one or two people violates the confidentiality of individual respondents.) As you work with group-level data, you should support the confidentiality of the data by establishing guidelines with the supervisor and group members regarding who may see the data and under what conditions.

As a consultant, your role in organizing the data begins once you receive data for groups you will be working with. You should become thoroughly acquainted with the high, low, and average aspects of the work group's functioning in order to present the data to the supervisor in a meaningful way. A thorough knowledge of the data will enable you to plan, with the group's supervisor, which issues to focus on in the work-group feedback meeting. The remaining sections of this module provide some concepts that will be useful in making sense of the work-group data, and strategies for helping the supervisor receive and understand his group's responses.

WORK-GROUP DATA PRINTOUT

When you receive a printout of data for an individual work group, it is reported in a format similar to that shown in Figure 5. This section provides some definitions of the terms included on the printout, so refer to Figure 5 as you study the following information. The numbers correspond to the numbered areas on the sample printout.

GROUP NUMBER 340

ITEM	PERCENTAGE DISTRIBUTION					MEAN	STD DEV.	N
	(1)	(2)	(3)	(4)	(5)			
7 CO USES NEW WK METHODS	0	6	75	6	13	3.25	0.75	16
8 CO INTEREST IN WELFARE	0	25	38	31	6	3.19	0.88	16
9 CO IMPROVES WKING COND	0	19	50	25	6	3.19	0.81	16
10 CO HAS CLEAR GOALS	6	6	50	31	6	3.25	0.90	16
11 WK ACTIVITY ORGANIZED	0	19	50	31	0	3.13	0.70	16
12 YOU GET OTH UNIT INFO	19	25	44	13	0	2.50	0.94	16

Figure 5.   Sample group data printout

1. *Group Number.* This is the number that was assigned to a particular supervisor. All people who report to the same supervisor put this number in the Supervisory Identification Grid (*00340*, the original five-digit number has been abbreviated here to *340*). This number indicates *which* work group's data is reported below.

2. *Item.* The survey question numbers and paraphrased labels are provided to help you identify items on which data is being reported. These labels save you the trouble of having to frequently refer to the complete text in the survey. (For example, question 7 stated fully is: "To what extent is this organization generally quick to use improved work methods?") Data for all items are reported in chronological order, followed by supplementary questions (if used). Following item scores, index scores are labeled, numbered, and reported in the same way.

3. *Percentage Distribution.* The response scale on each survey question (except demographics) is 1 to 5 as represented here. Under each number on the response scale, the percentage of the work-group respondents who chose each of the answer choices on a particular question is listed. The percentage distribution indicates the amount of agreement among group members on a particular question. For example, on question 7, 75 percent of the group chose answer 3 ("to some extent"), as compared to a scattering of choices among 2, 4, and 5. This indicates a higher amount of agreement among most group members on question 7 than is shown on question 8, where answers 2, 3, and 4 shared the bulk of responses.

4. *Mean.* The mean is simply the average response for the group members on the particular item or index. The mean score in combination with the percentage distribution gives information on the general feeling of the group. The mean alone is not representative of the group unless the percentage distribution shows that the group members are reasonably agreed in their response.

5. *Standard Deviation* (Std. Dev.). This is a statistical measure of the extent to which opinions of group members differ, on the average difference from the mean score. The greater the difference of opinion among members, the larger the standard deviation. You can also see the extent or opinion differences in groups by examining the percentage distribution.

6. *N.* The numbers in this column indicate the number of work-group members who responded to each question or the number of people who took the survey in the work group. The numbers may vary slightly on a few items, which indicates that someone left a question blank.

You must familiarize yourself with all these terms so that you can begin to make sense of the group's data. All items and indices for each individual work group will be listed out in the format exemplified by Figure 5.

STANDARD OF COMPARISON

Work-group data, as presented on the computer printout, tell *how* group members view the organization and their group's functioning. The supervisor and his subordinates will also want to know how *well* the group functions as they work with their data. To get this kind of information, work-group scores must be compared to scores of other people who have responded to the same survey. In other words, the group data are measured against a meaningful *standard of comparison*.

The first section of this module noted the distinction between systemic data and work-group data. Three examples of systemic data—data summarized over the whole organization, by functional or departmental area, and by hierarchical level—were identified. Each of these may serve as a standard of comparison against which work-group data may be measured. For example, if work-group data is compared with data from the whole organization, information is obtained about how well the group is doing relative to other groups surveyed at the same time and under similar conditions. Since both the work group and the standard are from the same organization in this case, both have some characteristics in common (e.g., aspects of organizational climate). However, a comparison of the group to the total system should take into account the system's level of effectiveness. If the whole organization has low scores, the work group may look good by comparison, even though it also has low scores. Or, if the whole organization has high scores, the work group may look low in comparison, even though its own scores are also high.

One way to lessen this problem is to compare the group data to *norms* that are based on scores from all individuals in all organizations who took the survey. Comparing the group to these norms cancels out problems that are specific to one organization and indicates the group's strengths or weaknesses in comparison to a much larger standard. The group may also want to see how well it is doing compared to other groups that have similar functions or are at the same hierarchical level. Functional or level norms across the whole norm group are the appropriate standard of comparison for obtaining this kind of information.

Several comparisons of the group data will give a more complete picture of the group. Remember, however, that too much information can be overwhelming for the supervisor and his subordinates and will detract from the usefulness of the data. It is better to choose the standard that will provide the most appropriate and specific information for the supervisor and work-group members.

Assume that you have chosen to compare the work group with norms that have been generated on all survey items and indices across all the organizations surveyed. These norms have been made available to you in the form of percentiles ranging from 0 to 100 percent. You want to know where the work group falls on this scale when its *mean* scores are compared with the norm mean scores. The result of this comparison is a percentile score. Figure 6 shows an example of how this comparison is made.

The example illustrates that, when compared to the norm, the work group's percentile score on supervisory support is 46. This means that the work-group score of 3.27 is higher than 46 percent of the groups included in the standard and lower than 54 percent of the groups. It is most important for you to understand that the percentile score indicates where the group falls in relation to the standard.

UNDERSTANDING AND ORGANIZING WORK-GROUP DATA

Comparing the data to a meaningful standard and obtaining percentile scores allows you to identify the strong and weak areas of a group's functioning. It is apparent that the scores farthest to the left (toward the 0 percent end) of the percentile scale are the lowest, and those farthest to the right (toward the 100 percent end) of the percentile scale are the highest. It may be less clear at this point which scores are considered as average. Generally, it is useful to designate the percentile range between the 40th and 60th percentiles as average. This range offers more flexibility than designating only one point, such as the 50th percentile, as average.

Interpreting Work-Group Scores

Assume that you are at the point of having a firm idea of which indices of the group data fall into low, average, and high percentile-score categories. Now, you must organize the data to describe the work group's functioning. The relationships among various areas measured by the survey provide essential clues for organizing the data.

Focus for a moment on five major areas that are measured by the Survey of Organizations: organizational climate, supervisory leadership, peer leadership, group process, and satisfaction. (See Module 2 for descriptions of indices and the items they include.) Research has shown that these five areas affect each other in a causal manner. In looking at work-group data, this means that each work group is affected

The index used in the example is Supervisory Support.
Here is how the norms might look for this index:

1.00	2.00	2.50	2.83	3.17	3.33	3.67	3.83	4.17	4.50	5.00
0	10	20	30	40	50	60	70	80	90	100*

*We have supplied these percentile labels to show you what the breakpoints mean as they are displayed on the norms. Since in most cases the answer alternatives on the survey are from 1 (1.00) to 5 (5.00) the 0 percentile = 1.00 and the 100 percentile = 5.00, and are not usually repeated on the norm sheet.

Suppose the work-group mean score for this index is 3.27. When this score is compared to the norm scale, it falls between 3.17 and 3.33, or between the 40th and 50th percentiles. To find the exact percentile of 3.27, follow these steps:

(1) Subtract 3.17 from 3.33   Answer: .16
(2) Subtract 3.17 from the group mean score, 3.27   Answer: .10
(3) Divide Answer (2), .10, by Answer (1), .16   Answer: .625

(4) Rounding answer (3), the group mean, 3.27, is .6 of
    the distance between 40 and 50, so the percentile
    score for 3.27 is 46.

Figure 6.

by the organizational climate within which it functions. Specifically, supervisory behavior in any one group is largely affected by the policies and conditions that make up the climate. For instance, if one of the supervisory-leadership indices is low, such as supervisory-goal emphasis, this may be partly because aspects of climate, such as communication flow, are low. Thus, the supervisor may not get the information he needs to help set goals and plan the group's work schedule adequately.

Group members often mirror the type of leadership shown by their supervisor. This means that if the supervisor does not help the group to set goals and to plan ahead, the peer-goal emphasis index may also be low. The planning done by peers is limited by the extent to which their supervisor provides the information and guidance they need to set goals among themselves. Although group members may try to make up for deficiencies in goal setting, their efforts may be confounded when they do not have all the information they need to plan realistically. Consequently, the group's functioning, as measured by the group-process index, suffers. Finally, since group members carry out their most meaningful interactions and activities within their work group, when group coordination is inadequate or frustrating, individual satisfaction may be adversely affected.

The flow of events shown in Figure 7 should indicate that low or high areas in the work-group data have varying effects, depending on their place in the causal chain. It should also help you to decide which areas the group has the most control over and can work on to improve.

An example is supervisory leadership, an area that has much direct influence on peer leadership and some indirect influence on group process and satisfaction. If the work group wanted to begin by focusing on low scores in group process, it would have to work back through the sequence and check out possible problem areas in supervisory leadership that may be affecting the group's function. If climate areas are low, this does not mean the group's efforts will prove fruitless, though climate is first in the causal chain. It means, rather, that the group must realistically assess the climate in which it functions and work to alleviate or work around the hindrances presented by the climate.

Interpreting work-group data according to the causal sequence enables you to discern relationships among important aspects of the work group's functioning. Such an understanding should help as you prepare to present and discuss the data in meetings with the supervisor and with the whole work group.

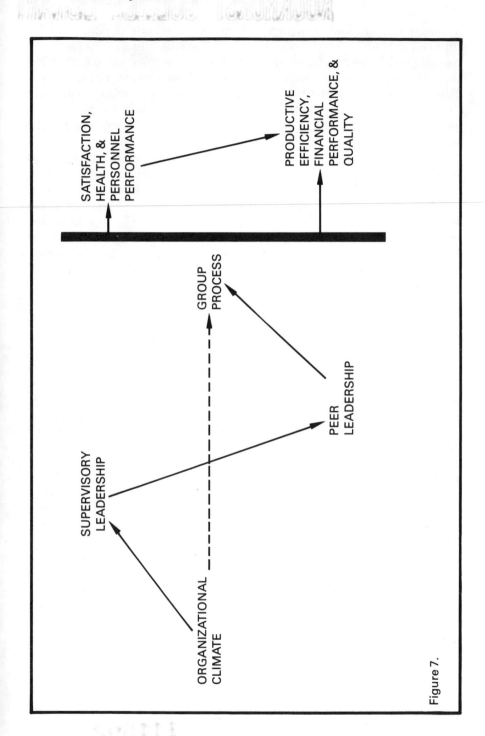

Figure 7.

Organizing Data for Feedback

As you begin to gain a thorough understanding of the work group's data, you also should consider how to meaningfully organize the data in order to facilitate the group's interpretation and use of the data. The causal sequence is a useful tool for understanding the data.

In preparing the data for use in meetings with the supervisor and the work group, you must also consider which aspects of the data may provide a motivating focus for the supervisor and the work group. This decision is made on the basis of the information gained in sorting through data scores. You may have found that overall, the work group roughly fits one of the following types: (1) all of the indices fall in the below-average (less than 40) percentile-score range; (2) all of the indices fall in the above-average (greater than 60) percentile score range; or (3) the index scores are mixed (a few may be somewhat above or below average) and tend to present an average (between 40 and 60) percentile-score picture.

Depending on the type of group you are working with, your strategy in presenting the data will vary slightly. Regardless of the group type, however, your main concern is to identify and maintain motivating discrepancies.

The importance of motivating discrepancies was mentioned in Module 1, which stated that a moderate discrepancy between actual and ideal functioning is generally most motivating. In looking at work-group data, this means that the gap between the actual score and the group's goal must be of an optimal size—neither too great nor too small—to provoke the group's motivation to change in any area. The group's goal may be represented by the standard of comparison, by scores reported on "ideal" survey items (see Module 2), or by how its members would like to see the group function—as reflected in a designated score level. A large discrepancy, as shown for instance by an area having a very low percentile score, may seem self-defeating. On the other hand, a very small discrepancy (for example, an average or above-average item) may be ignored as not worth the group's effort, or may suggest that the area may change by itself with time.

Referring back to the three types of groups previously mentioned, you may ask the question, "If most of the scores fall below the 40th percentile, does this mean that the data will present self-defeating or overwhelming discrepancies to the group?" It may seem to you that given this first type of group, the data may be scrapped by the group as not worth attention. This possibility is a reminder to always focus on the relative differences between the item and index scores in organizing the data. That is, even if all the scores cluster within the lower percentile range, there will be some areas that are closer to average than others. You should identify the motivating discrepancies in this instance by encouraging both the supervisor and group members to set goals in terms of the higher scoring areas. The group then plans to work toward bringing the lower areas up to or beyond the level of the relatively higher areas.

The same strategy would apply with a group of the second type, in which most scores fall in the above-average percentile range. The higher scoring areas represent a goal toward which other areas can be improved. It is particularly important in a group of this type, where the tendency is toward complacency, that you emphasize and maintain optimal discrepancies in this manner.

Perhaps the hardest set of data to deal with is the third type of group, in which all scores tend to cluster within the average range. One might expect that this kind of data would tend to produce apathy within the group, since it points neither to definite strengths nor to weaknesses. When the data are clustered in this manner, there are no built-in goals represented by higher areas toward which other areas may be improved. Therefore, you must help the group create its own motivating discrepancies by setting higher standards for itself. The group may realistically set goals using its own potential resources—which are substantiated by its average-scoring data—to build on. As you organize the data before sitting down with the supervisor, you must be well prepared to emphasize optimal discrepancies between the group's lower and higher areas of functioning or between actual scores and scores that the group feels would indicate its goal. Modules 4 and 5 cover the use of motivating discrepancies as a strategy in consultant meetings with work-group supervisors, and in work-group feedback meetings.

The level of scores shown in a work group's data may not be the only consideration, however, to be used in deciding the areas of functioning in which the group members will be motivated to improve. The present energy level of the group will, of course, influence group members' reactions to and subsequent use of the data. Before receiving their data, some groups may already have in mind areas they would like to work on, or improve. And for some groups, the greatest discrepancy from the goal, or the lowest-scoring areas, may capture their attention and incite the greatest motivation to change. If this is the case, it may not be effective for you to insistently focus only on moderate-sized discrepancies that you have noted in particular areas, because the group may be motivated to work on problem areas other than these. In guiding the group's productive use of its data, however, you must be cautious in discriminating when an area is important to the group's functioning, and worth the group's effort. Problems in any part of the causal sequence are indicators of areas important to the group's effectiveness. Therefore, you should capitalize on the group's motivation level and maintain it while exercising caution in keeping their energy productively channeled.

DATA PREPARATION AND DISPLAY

Thus far, this module has focused on ways of organizing the group data after you receive the printout. At this point in the procedure, you should have a fairly good grasp of group strengths and weaknesses. You probably also have cited areas where improvements could be made, based on the motivating discrepancies suggested by the data. Now your task is to present the data to the supervisor, enabling him to understand the major features of the data. This means that the data must be further organized and simplified in order for the supervisor and work group to readily use them without having to repeat all the steps you have already carried out. Preparing visual data displays is the most efficient way of clearly presenting a good deal of information. The way you group the data for display will depend on the information you have obtained in organizing them.

Data displays serve several important functions. By highlighting major features, they greatly facilitate the job of presenting the data. In grouping related indices together, displays allow you to clearly present information about relationships among scores. In addition, displays reinforce the notion of the standard of comparison and show how the percentile score is obtained. Finally, by displaying the data, you provide a visual and content focus around which discussion may be organized by the supervisor and group members.

Figure 8 presents a sample profile chart that fulfills these purposes. As shown, all leadership measures have been grouped together, which facilitates the group's understanding of how scores on supervisory and peer leadership interact. The chart illustrates aspects of the percentile scale that would be difficult to explain in any other manner. First, the farther to the right an index score is, the greater the group's strength in that area, as compared to the standard. As shown, however, the standard percentile scale changes with each index. This means if one looks at the first two indices (supervisory support and supervisory work facilitation), that a mean score of 3.80 on support attains a lower percentile score (about 45) than a mean score of 3.62 on work facilitation, which is at the 69th percentile. This example emphasizes the fact that percentile rather than mean scores should be the major focus of attention. In talking with the supervisor, you must be prepared to stress the usefulness of the percentile scores and the information they supply.

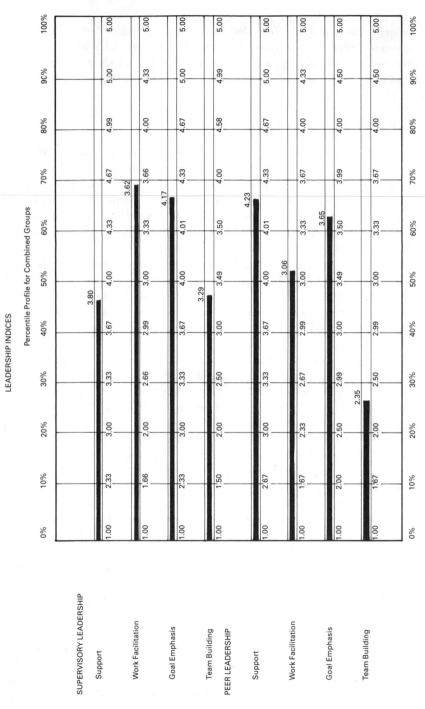

Figure 8. Sample profile chart

Figure 9 provides another example of displaying the same data. In this example, the relationship between the indices is even more emphasized. The extent to which the plotted scores form a round circle indicates the degree to which leadership is well balanced and equally shared by supervisors and work-group members. It also suggests the extent to which skills in all four leadership behaviors—support, work facilitation, goal emphasis, and team building—are equally present. A lopsided wheel suggests leadership styles that result from various combinations of strong and weak points in the four leadership areas.

As you study these displays, note the importance of clearly labeling charts and presenting enough, but not too much, information on any one chart. In addition, the standard group to which the group's data are compared should be mentioned on the chart. You and the supervisor should also decide how to present your charts to enable all group members to have visual access to the displays in group meetings. Duplicate copies may be made, or charts may be presented via projection. Finally, you may want to enlist the supervisor's help in preparing the charts in order to increase his own understanding of the data. Again, the goal of data display is to further organize the data and to enhance the supervisor's and group members' understanding of them.

GROUP-DATA FEEDBACK PACKAGE

An underlying theme of this module has been the notion that you must organize the group data in a meaningful way in order to present them to the group's supervisor. The supervisor should understand much of the information presented thus far. Although going through all of the steps you have carried out in organizing the data may not be necessary, the supervisor needs enough information to feel comfortable in presenting the data to his subordinates. Preferably, the supervisor should be familiar with the computer printout and the items included in the various indices before actually receiving the group's data and being faced with the task of understanding them and presenting them to the group. Part of your role is to provide the supervisor with at least this minimal amount of preparation. An efficient way to accomplish this is by compiling a standard feedback package that can be used as a reference by the supervisor. A standard feedback package would also lessen the time you need to spend in organizing and explaining the data. It may contain some material about the questionnaire structure, content, and purpose, as well as suggestions for using the data.

The content of the feedback package represents a simplified version of the practical skills you have been learning that are directly related to interpreting the data. In getting this information together, there are several essential areas that you should focus upon:

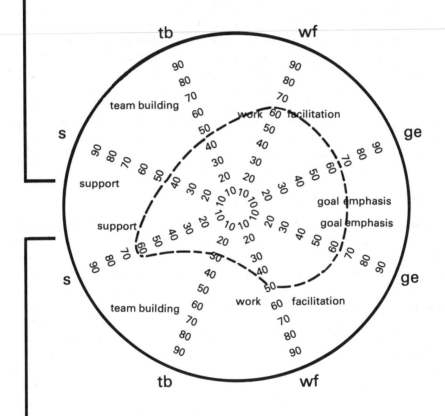

Figure 9. Leadership percentile wheel

- A brief, generalized description of the purpose of the survey, focusing upon the work group's involvement in the survey-guided development process (see Modules 1 and 2);
- Suggestions for how to use the work-group data, once they have been received (see Modules 3, 4, and 5);
- Definitions of terms such as work group, leadership, and organizational climate (see Modules 2 and 3);
- A description of what the survey measures and how, including a list of indices and the survey items they include (see Module 2);
- A description of computer-printout format and statistical terms (see Module 3); and
- Information on ways in which data may be graphically displayed (see Module 3).

When you provide such a standard package before the supervisor receives the data, his own involvement with the effort as a whole may increase. He can assume some responsibility for familiarizing himself with the nature of the data. Consequently, as his confidence in interpreting and presenting the data grows, apprehensions that he may have about receiving and using his group's data are lessened. Use of the feedback package also reduces the time you must spend explaining the data format to the supervisor. You can then focus data interpretation in planning for the work-group meeting.

Module 4
Meeting with Work-Group Supervisor

After the consultant has had a chance to look at and understand a particular work group's data, he then holds a meeting with the group's supervisor. This meeting has several purposes:

1. To share the data with the supervisor;
2. To bring problems, as indicated by the data and where motivating discrepancies exist, to the supervisor's attention;
3. To get the supervisor committed to sharing the data with the members of his work group; and
4. To plan a work-group meeting for discussing the data and identifying and solving problems.

The last two points here are extremely important, because any subsequent efforts by the work group to use the survey data and to solve its problems require the support and leadership of the supervisor. Therefore, this first meeting between the consultant and the supervisor is crucial for establishing that support and commitment.

PREPARATION FOR THE MEETING

To adequately prepare for the meeting with the supervisor, the consultant should have studied the data according to procedures discussed in Module 3. By using the appropriate standard of comparison, you should have identified the group's strengths and weaknesses and any optimal-sized motivating discrepancies the data indicate. You should also have some idea of the areas that should be initially focused on in terms of their position in the causal flow of events and the presence of optimal discrepancies.

Finally, you should have made some decisions about appropriate ways of displaying the work-group data. You will be presenting those data to the supervisor in this meeting and should have some displays prepared for that purpose. You should also be prepared to make some recommendations concerning how the data will be displayed to the work group members.

PHASES OF THE MEETING

A note about format: for each phase of the meeting to be discussed with the work-group supervisor, three kinds of information are given. First, there are some general notes about the kinds of issues with which that phase of the meeting is concerned. Some examples of the kinds of things that happen during that phase are presented.

After this general information, there is a listing of events that are expected and that should happen during that phase of the meeting. You might consider these as guidelines for a good meeting. If they do not occur, the consultant should try to judge whether the activities that are occurring are appropriate, given the objectives of the meeting. If they are not, you should be prepared to step in and convey the necessary information or encourage the appropriate behavior.

Finally, a second set of events is listed for each phase; namely, those things that might happen during a meeting and that should be dealt with if they do. You might consider these problems that should be avoided in a good meeting. If these things occur, the consultant should once again step in and provide information or make suggestions on how the meeting might continue. After each such item, one or more key words are listed (e.g., **confidentiality; consultant role**). These key words refer to the techniques, that is, the information and skills that the consultant might use in the situation described. These techniques are defined and illustrated in Module 9 and can be referenced by their key words.

Phase 1: Starting the Meeting

GENERAL OVERVIEW

The nature of this initial meeting has a great deal of influence on the way in which the data is subsequently presented and used in the work-group feedback meeting. Therefore, it is crucial that the consultant set the meeting as well as the data he presents in the proper perspective for the supervisor. You should be aware that the supervisor may be worried about the data or confused about the feedback effort in general and his role in particular. In answering his questions, your goal is to encourage accurate expectations for upcoming activities.

THINGS THAT *SHOULD* HAPPEN

1. The consultant should relate this meeting to the total survey-guided development effort. You should review the goal of the total effort and the activities that have gone on so far. You also should explain some of the events that will follow, such as the work-group meeting, problem identification and solution efforts, future surveys, etc. As part of this background, you should briefly explain your role as a consultant in the effort.

2. You should discuss the goals of this particular meeting, that is, to help the supervisor understand his work group's data and to prepare for the work-group meeting where the data will be fed back.

THINGS THAT *MIGHT* HAPPEN

1. The supervisor may have a negative attitude toward the entire program of which the survey is a part. He may resist taking any role in it whatsoever.

> **Info:**   **goals of the effort;**
> **how one-on-one meeting fits**
> **in effort;**
>
> **Skills:**   **dealing with resistance**

2. The supervisor may not want the data fed back to him at all. This may be due to anxiety or disinterest.

> **Info:**   **goals of the effort;**
>
> **Skills:**   **confidentiality;**
> **dealing with resistance**

3. The supervisor may only want the consultant to drop off the data but not discuss it. He may promise to "take a look at it later."

> **Info:**   **what the data mean;**
> **how one-on-one meeting fits**
> **in effort**

4. The supervisor may resist the idea of holding a work group meeting. He may feel that it is unnecessary because the data and any indicated problems are his responsibility.

> **Info:**   **source of the data;**
> **value of group problem**
> **solving;**
>
> **Skills:**   **dealing with resistance**

Phase 2: Feeding Back the Data

GENERAL OVERVIEW

In going through the work-group data with the supervisor, you should proceed at a slow enough pace to avoid overwhelming the supervisor. You should explain the various terms and format that are used and encourage the supervisor to ask questions. Often, because you have carefully gone through the data, things appear obvious to you that are confusing to a person seeing them for the first time. As mentioned in Module 3, a group-data feedback package, if one has been devised, can be an enormous help in increasing the supervisor's understanding of the data. And any data displays you have prepared can clarify the data.

THINGS THAT *SHOULD* HAPPEN

1. The consultant should explain the source of the data by defining "work group" and how the data were combined.
2. The consultant should emphasize the confidentiality of the data and explain who will have access to them. You should point out that it is impossible to identify individual responses.
3. The consultant should explain the format of the data printout and what the various entries mean. (See Module 3.)
4. The consultant should define the various items and indices, referring to the Survey of Organizations as necessary.
5. The consultant should explain the idea of using standards of comparison in looking at data. You should discuss any that you have used in preparing data displays for this meeting and the reasons for their use. You should make sure the supervisor understands any displays he is shown.
6. If a group-data feedback package has been prepared, the consultant should refer to it and show the supervisor how to use it as a reference as he continues to work with his group's data.

THINGS THAT *MIGHT* HAPPEN

1. The supervisor may deny or reject the data. He may claim that the survey was filled out on "a bad day." He may concentrate on the mean scores rather than on percentiles.

   Info: **source of the data;**
             norms;

   Skills: **dealing with resistance**

2. The supervisor may not consider the data valid. He may question the validity of the survey itself. He may claim that his work group is unique and that a standard survey cannot accurately assess it.

> **Info: Survey of Organizations;**
> **source of data;**
> **norms**

3. The supervisor may get confused about particular items or indices. He may not understand how they interrelate.

> **Info: Survey of Organizations;**
> **group-data feedback**
> **package**

4. The supervisor may want to know how particular individuals answered. He may try to infer patterns of responses, especially from the percentage distribution section of the printout.

> **Skills: confidentiality**

5. The supervisor may want to know how other work groups answered or how his data compared to some other supervisor's.

> **Skills: confidentiality**

Phase 3:   Discussing Strengths and Weaknesses

GENERAL OVERVIEW

Because receiving as much information as the data provide can be a confusing and sometimes overwhelming experience, the consultant should be able to provide the supervisor with perceptions of any trends that the data may indicate. This will help organize and make sense of the data for the supervisor. This especially may be needed if the supervisor is faced with low supervisory leadership scores. These scores may be all he can focus on and you should draw his attention to other areas of the data.

It is important to point out a work group's strengths, as well as its weaknesses. In order to successfully build up weak spots, a grasp of which and where strong points can be capitalized on is needed.

In sharing your perceptions of the data, you should avoid diagnosing the work group or hypothesizing cause-effect relationships. Your discussion should be merely descriptive and concentrate on task-related issues.

THINGS THAT *SHOULD* HAPPEN

1. The consultant should point out strengths as well as weaknesses that are indicated by the data. If necessary, the notion of standards of comparison should be explained again.

2. The consultant should discuss any problem areas or issues according to the priorities set during the preparation for this meeting. That is, areas should be discussed in terms of their position in the causal flow of events and the presence of an optimal motivating discrepancy.

3. The consultant should concentrate his discussion on issues relating to how well the group accomplishes its task. Discussing a problem in terms of how well individuals get along together should be avoided unless it bears directly on task performance. You should encourage the supervisor to think of examples of these issues that occur on the job.

THINGS THAT *MIGHT* HAPPEN

1. The supervisor may try to diagnose his work group. He may try to interpret the data or find causes for the various problems raised.
   > **Skills:** **sticking to the data;**
   > **separation of P/I and P/S**

2. The supervisor may try to pinpoint problems in terms of solutions that he himself can develop and apply. He may do this because he thinks it is his responsibility or because he does not want the problems to be raised with the work group.
   > **Info:** **value of group problem**
   > **solving**

3. The supervisor may deny that problems exist. He may claim that the problem areas raised are meaningless because the data are invalid. He may misunderstand how indices are constructed from items. He may feel that overall his data are positive or the "best possible" picture and that they cannot or need not change.
   > **Info:** **source of the data;**
   > **group-data feedback package;**
   > **Skills:** **identifying motivating**
   > **discrepancies**

4. The supervisor may focus on problems that he sees as relating to differences among a few individuals. He may try to find out who the "troublemakers" are. This may be an attempt to conceal a larger problem the supervisor is unwilling to face.
   > **Skills:** **staying task-oriented;**
   > **confidentiality;**
   > **objectifying problems**

5. The supervisor may get disillusioned or defensive about the problem areas raised. This is especially likely to occur about supervisory leadership practices.

Skills: sticking to the data

6. The supervisor may want problem areas identified but his behavior may imply that he has no intention of following through with a group problem-solving effort. This may be due to disinterest or apprehension.

**Info: how one-on-one meeting fits
              in effort;
              value of group problem
              solving**

Phase 4: Planning for the Work-Group Feedback Meeting

GENERAL OVERVIEW

In survey-guided development, it is expected that at some point work-group data will be fed back to those who generated it, that is, the members of the work group themselves. To do this, all the members of the work group must meet together. This is a crucial step for generating successful solutions to the problems that the data indicate as being faced by the work group. Solutions and action plans that are developed by the group itself, rather than being imposed on it, will be most effective. Group members will be more committed to carrying out their own plans. In addition, group-devised plans should be adequately and accurately designed to meet the group's own needs and use its resources.

Although, ideally, the consultant attends this work-group feedback meeting, the supervisor should take primary responsibility for it. To this end, you should help the supervisor plan for the group meeting, and be available as a resource to the supervisor.

THINGS THAT *SHOULD* HAPPEN

1. The consultant should discuss the purpose and function of the work-group meeting. He should explain that the data ought to be returned to their source, the group members. Also the supervisor should be told the potential benefits of a work group identifying and solving its own problems.

2. The supervisor should schedule the meeting. Ideally it should be held at a time when the consultant and all work-group members can

attend. The supervisor should arrange for whatever notification is necessary and for a location for the meeting.

3. Expectations should be set regarding the role of the consultant and the role of the supervisor in the meeting. The supervisor should clearly understand that he will be leading the meeting and that the consultant will be there as a resource to the whole group and to provide any needed support.

4. The supervisor and consultant should decide on what data to provide the work group and what form those data should take. That is, an appropriate standard of comparison and data display format should be agreed on. The consultant should encourage the supervisor to provide a full range of the data, that is, not only the particularly positive or particularly negative data, but an adequate representation of the total picture the data present. On the other hand, providing extremely detailed forms of the data will probably be more confusing than useful to the work group as a whole. Appropriate display formats can be used to make the data more easily understood by the work group.

5. The supervisor and consultant should prepare an agenda for the work-group meeting. Some items that should be covered include: (a) introduction of the consultant, (b) data feedback, (c) general areas to be discussed, (d) problem identification, and (e) problem-solving discussions.

6. The consultant should explain the processes of problem identification and problem solving. The supervisor especially should understand the phases of an effective problem-solving discussion so that he can lead such a discussion during the work-group meeting. These phases are (1) defining the problem, (2) generating solutions, (3) evaluating solutions, (4) selecting a solution, (5) building action steps, and (6) planning for review. These phases are more fully defined in Module 5.

7. The consultant and supervisor should discuss any questions about procedures or the kinds of issues that may arise during the work-group meeting. The consultant should inquire about any concerns the supervisor may have about difficulties that may arise during the meeting, for example, if a few people reject the data or turn the meeting into an unproductive gripe session. Together the consultant and supervisor should brainstorm possible tactics to use in such situations, such as staying task-oriented and sticking to the data. The consultant should make it clear that he will intervene in the discussion only if he thinks it is needed.

THINGS THAT *MIGHT* HAPPEN

1. The supervisor may put off scheduling the meeting. In some cases he may do this because he honestly does not have the information he needs to arrange a time. In other cases, however, he may be resisting the idea of holding the meeting.

   Info: how group-feedback meeting fits in effort

2. The supervisor may try to get the consultant to run the work group meeting. He may do this because he feels uneasy about handling the discussion of the data or problems. On the other hand, this may be an attempt to remove himself from the feedback process and from any problems that may be identified by the group.

   Info: consultant role

3. The supervisor may not want the consultant to attend the work-group meeting. The consultant's response to this must be contingent on the perceived importance of this group in the organization and the amount of time available. If the group is crucial and the consultant could attend the meeting, he should try to attend.

   Info: dealing with resistance;

   Skills: maintaining a systemic perspective

4. The supervisor may resist feeding data back to the work group. He may do this because he feels the information need not or should not be shared. He may not want data about himself made available. This may be due to disappointment or to a fear about the consequences of sharing this data, for example, that a bad image of him will spread throughout the organization. Also the supervisor may be unwilling to change his behavior in the ways the data indicate he should.

   Info: value of feedback

   Skills: dealing with resistance

5. The supervisor may resist providing the data in terms of a standard of comparison. He may want to focus on the absolute mean values of the items or indices.

   Info: value of standards of comparison

6. The supervisor may resist discussing problems with his work group. He may be resisting the idea of group problem solving. He may feel that any problems that the group may have are his responsibility and that it is his job to solve them himself. He may not want the group to

share their ideas of what problems exist, saying either that they will get discouraged or that they will just create more problems.

> **Info:**   **source of the data;**
> **value of group problem**
> **solving**

Phase 5: Closing the Meeting

At the close of the meeting with the work-group supervisor, the consultant should briefly review some of the points that have been covered. You should confirm when the work-group meeting is scheduled and what the proposed agenda will be. You should encourage the supervisor to study his work group's data thoroughly. Finally, you should let the supervisor know how to contact you before the work-group meeting in case he has any additional questions.

Module 5
Work-Group Feedback Meeting

This module is designed to answer several questions, including:

1. Why have work-group feedback meetings?
2. What happens at a group-feedback meeting?
3. What does the consultant do at these meetings?

WHY HAVE WORK-GROUP FEEDBACK MEETINGS?

A work-group feedback meeting has three general purposes: (1) to share survey data with work-group members, (2) to identify specific problems the data suggest, and (3) to take action to solve those problems. The consultant, supervisor, and all work-group members attend the meeting, even if they did not fill out the survey. Because the supervisor leads the meeting, he and his consultant should plan for it. (See Module 4.)

Several factors contribute to meaningful and successful feedback meetings. One is maintaining a focus on the group's tasks and the conditions hindering their accomplishment. The problem-solving activities the group undertakes may need the whole group's cooperation in order to succeed. Focusing on issues that group members face in common, rather than on personal differences between two or three people, encourages that cooperation. Often, identifying task-related problems and working to solve them can relieve the stresses that cause problems among people.

Group meetings will be more effective if you, as the consultant, do all you can to make sure the supervisor leads the group discussion. Doing so will emphasize the meeting as an activity being carried out by the work group with its supervisor. Ideally, this meeting should be very similar to the usual work situation, that is, with the supervisor leading the activities and the members doing the "work." This encourages people to try things they learn in these meetings, such as recognizing problems and solving them together, in the more usual work situation as well. In contrast, if the members see the meeting as a kind of sideshow put on by the consultant, they may ignore what occurs in the meeting. If the consultant is seen as engineering the activities, the members see the identified problems and generated solutions as someone else's. If the supervisor and the group lead and control the discussion, the members are more likely to feel committed to carrying out any proposed actions. Consequently, the consultant should act merely as a facilitator, providing information and intervening only when necessary for the group's effective progression through the meeting.

A clear understanding of how these group meetings fit in the total survey-guided development effort and how the present activities relate to meeting the effort's objectives helps to maintain both a task-oriented and group-owned emphasis in these meetings. Therefore, the consultant and supervisor must understand the total process and work to convey that appreciation to group members.

The sections of this module that follow describe the phases of a work-group feedback meeting, along with some ideas of what *should* happen, what *might* happen, and what you could do in either case.

PHASES OF THE WORK-GROUP FEEDBACK MEETING

A note about format: for each phase of the work-group feedback meeting to be discussed, three kinds of information are given. First, there are some general notes about the kinds of issues with which that phase of the meeting is concerned. Some examples of the kinds of things that happen during that phase are presented.

After this general information, there is a listing of events that are expected and that should happen during that phase of the meeting. You might consider these guidelines for a good meeting. If they do not occur, the consultant should try to judge whether the activities that are occurring are appropriate, given the objectives of the meeting. If they are not, you should be prepared to step in and convey the necessary information or encourage the appropriate behavior.

Finally, a second set of events is listed for each phase; namely, those things that might happen during a meeting and that should be dealt with if they do. You might consider these as problems that should be avoided in a good meeting. If these things occur, the consultant should once again step in and provide information or make suggestions on how the meeting might continue. After each such item, one or more key words are listed (e.g., **confidentiality; consultant role**). These key words refer to the techniques, that is, the information and skills that the consultant might use in the situation described. These techniques are defined and illustrated in Module 9 and can be referenced by their key words.

Phase 1:   Introduction of the Meeting

GENERAL OVERVIEW

The first phase of the meeting, its introduction, is very important because it provides an opportunity for insuring that organization members understand and accept their real responsibility for making the development effort a success. Indeed, if work-group members fail to gain this perspective, the organization loses its crucial building block for the effort, the commitment and action of its members.

Work group members typically come to this feedback meeting with many questions on their minds. "What are we meeting for?" "Does this have anything to do with that survey we filled out?" "Is our supervisor going to be handing down information or decisions from the top of the organization?" The consultant and supervisor should anticipate these kinds of questions and take steps to provide useful information to the work group when the meeting begins.

THINGS THAT *SHOULD* HAPPEN

1. The supervisor should clarify that this work group meeting is being held to feed back the survey data generated by this group. This is especially important if the work group holds other meetings for other reasons.

2. The supervisor should explain how this group-feedback meeting is part of an organization-wide development effort. He might give a brief description of the steps and activities involved in this effort.

3. The supervisor should introduce the consultant and explain what he will be doing at the meeting; for example, answering questions about the survey, the data, and the development effort, or making suggestions about how the group might improve the way that the meeting is going and that problems are being handled.

4. The supervisor should state the objectives of this feedback meeting. He should give the work-group members some idea of the things they will be doing during the meeting; for example, discussing the data, sharing perceptions of what goes on in the organization and their work group, identifying strengths and weaknesses of the work group, and working to solve problems that the group identifies.

5. The supervisor should close the introduction with a short description of the kinds of things that may happen in future meetings (for example, continued problem solving, reporting back on how well solutions have worked, setting new goals for the work group, etc.) and ask for any questions about this meeting.

THINGS THAT *MIGHT* HAPPEN

1. The supervisor may want the consultant to run the meeting. He may indicate this by continually asking you about what to do next.

   Skills: clarifying consultant's role

2. Group members may feel that the consultant is spying on their work group and will report back to the brass. You may sense this through their attitude when you are introduced or make any inputs, or some members may actually confront you with it.

   Info: consultant role;

   Skills: confidentiality

Phase 2: Discussion of the Data

GENERAL OVERVIEW

Prior to this meeting, the supervisor will have made some decisions, probably with the consultant's help, concerning what data to give the group and how to display those data. (See Modules 3 and 4.) During this phase, it is important for the work group to discuss how the data relate to the ways it accomplishes its tasks. Work-group members should be encouraged to share their perceptions of what helps and what hinders that accomplishment. Focusing on behaviors, that is, on the things people actually *do* on the job helps maintain this task perspective. To do this, the supervisor can read the survey items in the index being discussed and ask work-group members to describe the kinds of things they were thinking about when they answered those questions and to provide specific examples if they can. The examples might illustrate strengths as well as weaknesses.

THINGS THAT *SHOULD* HAPPEN

1. The supervisor should explain the source of the data, that is, that they are the summarized responses of all work-group members who filled out the survey. He should clarify that it is not possible to identify individual answers.

2. The supervisor should explain who has access to this work group's data. The consultant may be called on to provide specific information about how combined data are being handled in the organization. Ideally, only the supervisor, the consultant, and the work-group members would have access to the data. If someone higher in the organization receives data summarized for all the work groups beneath him, it would not be possible to separate out the answers of any particular work group, much less any particular

individual. If for some reason, the work group wanted other members of the organization to have access to the data, they could release their data.

3. As the data are reviewed, the supervisor should clearly define the various indices and items being discussed. A group-data feedback package would be a useful resource here. The supervisor should also explain norms, percentiles, and methods of comparison as required.

4. The supervisor should focus on areas where motivating discrepancies have been identified for this group.

THINGS THAT *MIGHT* HAPPEN

1. Work-group members may deny or reject the data. They may claim that they filled out the survey "on a bad day." They may ignore the percentile scores and concentrate on the absolute mean values for the items and indices, saying that "We said we were fairly satisfied with it" or whatever, though the percentile score is low. Individuals may argue that *they* did not answer that way and so reject the data. Sometimes the supervisor may do these things, too.

> **Info: source of the data; norms;**
>
> **Skills: dealing with resistance**

2. Work-group members of the supervisor may not see the data as valid. The validity of the survey instrument itself may be questioned. Others may argue that the picture of the work group that the data reflect is not valid. They may claim that their situation is unique, or that "Things aren't so bad as those numbers make it look."

> **Info: Survey of Organizations; source**
> **of the data; norms;**
>
> **Skills: dealing with resistance**

3. There may be confusion about particular indices or items. The supervisor or group members may need some clarification. The relationships among items and indices may need to be explained. It is important that group members realize that the number used to represent any one item can ultimately be tied back to perceptions they had about the behaviors that the survey item brought to mind as they completed the survey.

> **Info: group-data feedback package**

4. The supervisor or group members may want information about

other groups. They may want to know how their data compare to those from similar groups in the same unit. They may want to compare their data to similar groups in other units.

Info: norms;

Skills: confidentiality

5. The supervisor may try to find out what answers particular group members made, or he may try to discover who in the group gave a particular answer. He may do this by confronting the whole group ("Who answered to a very little extent on this question?") or he may confront individuals ("How do you feel about this, Stokes?")

Skills: confidentiality

6. The supervisor or group members may question the consultant for his own views about the content of the discussion, that is, the particular behaviors or problems or issues being discussed. This is especially likely to occur if there are conflicting points of view about a particular content issue. The people who are taking one stand may try to get the consultant to side with them by making a statement that supports their position. If you are seen as having expertise or some special power by virtue of your position, your statement will tend to add weight to their argument. Even if you personally have a strong commitment to a particular issue, it is *not* part of your role in a survey-guided development effort to take subjective stands.

Skills: staying objective

7. A few group members may tend to dominate the meeting. Every time the group discusses a particular item or issue, the same people may do all the talking. This tendency should be watched for during all phases of the work-group meeting.

Skills: gatekeeping

8. The discussion may get sidetracked. A particular item or particular example someone gives to illustrate some behavior may trigger a long series of anecdotes that get further and further from the issue at hand. This is especially likely to occur if members of the group have served in many different units. Hearing the horror stories that have taken place elsewhere can lead people to think they have no problems in comparison. Similarly, hearing how well another unit or work group worked together can lead people to believe there is no hope for their own work group. Once again, this sidetracking can occur at all phases of the meeting.

Skills: sticking to the data

9. The discussion may focus heavily on problems that have to do with how work-group members relate to each other on a personal level. While these kinds of issues can be very important to a group, they should be raised in the context of how they affect the group in accomplishing its task. The group may lose sight of the task in their discussion if it is allowed to get too focused on nontask issues. This, too, may occur at other phases in the meeting.

**Skills: staying task-oriented
sticking to the data**

10. Personality conflicts between members of the group may arise. One member may constantly interrupt another, or make snide remarks or subtle, cutting statements about or to another person. Usually the person will be under attack, rather than what he is saying. Perhaps "attack" is too strong a word; these conflicts are usually very subtle and an out-and-out confrontation may be rare. You should watch for them at all phases of the meeting, however.

**Skills: handling conflicts or
misunderstandings;
staying task-oriented;
sticking to the data**

11. The consultant may sense subtle efforts to resist or undermine the total effort. These may be made by members of the group or the supervisor. People may gloss over the data, discussing and appearing to accept them at an extremely rapid pace. On the other hand, there may be an extremely low level of energy in the group, in which everyone appears to have a "don't care" attitude and merely agrees half-heartedly to try things that you suggest.

**Info: goals of the effort;
how group-feedback meeting
fits in effort;**

Skills: dealing with resistance

Phase 3: Problem Identification

GENERAL OVERVIEW

In this phase of the meeting, using the survey data as a basis, the group identifies problems that need to be solved. The data may suggest areas of weakness that the group can further clarify and define as problems. The discussion should be kept as specific as possible.

This step in the problem-solving process should be kept separate from later stages, such as solution generation or solution evaluation.

Initially, all problems that surface in the group should be acknowledged and recorded. After many such problems have been identified, group members should decide which are most important to them. Problems that the group considers unimportant or not feasible to solve may be postponed from further immediate consideration. The supervisor should encourage group members to focus on task-related problems that they face in common, rather than on personal differences among two or three people. Also, the group should separate problems within its control, that is, those it can solve, from those outside its control. They can work on solving the former and refer the latter to the appropriate groups. Finally, from his knowledge of the data, the supervisor can focus on certain problems where motivating discrepancies are optimal.

THINGS THAT *SHOULD* HAPPEN

1. The group should identify its strengths as well as its weaknesses. Groups can get discouraged concentrating on the problems they have to cope with. This should be balanced with attention to areas where the group functions effectively.

2. The group should identify problems. Particular low indices or items may stimulate a discussion of the reasons for the weakness. This may take one of two directions. The group may be able to generally or vaguely define a problem ("We don't communicate."). Group members should be encouraged to narrow the problem down somewhat ("Is communication bad among group members and the supervisor, among group members, or among work groups?"), and finally to give a few specific examples of the problem ("Yesterday, no one told me about the maintenance-schedule change."). On the other hand, the group may be able to respond to a particular item with specific examples ("Smitty never told me that the maintenance work was done."), and should then be encouraged to characterize that as a more general problem—("Communication among group members is inadequate."). Both kinds of problem definition should go on. The general description provides a frame of reference; the specific examples clarify it.

3. The supervisor or a work-group member should keep a record of the identified problems.

4. After problems have been initially presented and listed, the group should decide which to work on first. Problems that are perceived by at least several members of the group and occur frequently should get high priority, rather than issues that trouble only one or two people or occur very rarely. Of those common problems, those

the group considers most important or easiest to solve should be listed first. The group should be kept focused on task-related problems and should identify those problems in terms of their effect on how the group accomplishes its task.

5. The group should separate problems it can solve from problems it cannot control. When a problem is not within the control of the work-group, it should identify who does have control over that area. The supervisor should agree to refer that problem to the group who controls it and report back to this group.

6. For the problems within this group's control, the supervisor should focus attention on and encourage high priority for those with an optimal-sized motivating discrepancy. Choosing to work on problems where the gap is too big becomes self-defeating when only a little progress can be made. On the other hand, working on areas where present levels are close to a desirable level becomes something of an artificial exercise. The ground between these very large and very small gaps is the most fertile for generating workable and motivating problem-solving activities.

THINGS THAT *MIGHT* HAPPEN

1. The group may not be able to get started at this phase. Group members may be silent for quite a while. The supervisor at this point could begin posting problems himself.

    Skills: posting; dealing with silence

2. The group members may say "We don't have any problems." Group members may say this as a comparison to other work groups they know about that are worse off. They may be trying to avoid confronting some issues.

    Skills: identifying motivating discrepancies; dealing with resistance

3. The group may feel it has so many problems that it does not know where to start. The group may begin to resist this phase of the meeting and feel that the effort is hopeless.

    Skills: prioritizing problems

4. The group may see many problems in terms of the personalities involved. Group members may lose sight of how the problems interfere with accomplishing a task. They may start to blame particular group members unjustifiably.

> **Skills: objectifying problems;**
> **staying task-oriented;**
> **sticking to the data**

5. The supervisor or group members may say that a particular problem cannot be solved by this group or anyone else. They may start giving all the reasons why it is unsolvable and cannot be changed. They may sometimes do this in an effort to bury a problem.

> **Skills: separation of P/I and P/S**

6. The supervisor or group members may offer solutions to problems in this phase of the meeting. They may offer to "take care of that." In those cases where the problem can be very easily and sensibly solved by one person, this can be very helpful and such indications of support for the problem-solving effort should be encouraged. In other cases, however, where the nature of the problem requires the group's cooperation for its solution, such offers may mask an effort to bury a problem.

> **Skills: separation of P/I and P/S**

7. People may be arguing and not hearing each other. They may be talking about completely different issues. They may actually be in agreement and simply not recognize it.

> **Skills: handling conflict and**
> **misunderstandings**

8. The supervisor or group members may get defensive about a particular problem being raised. They may feel that the group is blaming them, especially if they are used to illustrate a problem. They may try to claim that the issue is not a problem or that the group is being unfair.

> **Skills: objectifying problems;**
> **staying task-oriented**

9. The group may not see any payoff for participating in this phase of the meeting. Group members may feel this activity is a way to get them to air their gripes so that the brass can be told who the "troublemakers" are. They may feel that nothing will be done about the problems once they are identified.

> **Info: how group-feedback meeting fits**
> **in effort;**
> **Skills: confidentiality**

10. Members may feel that there are already mechanisms for reporting problems and airing grievances. They may question the reasons for meeting as a group.

Info: value of group problem solving

11. The supervisor may dominate this phase of the meeting. He may be quick to dismiss proposed problems as unimportant. He may want to post problems only if he agrees that they are problems. In order to fend off problems, he may try to control the meeting when data about him are being discussed.

**Skills: gatekeeping;
separation of P/I and P/S**

12. The group may spend too long a time on one issue or problem. Different members may continue to offer specific examples long after a common frame of reference has been established. Or the issue of whether a problem *is* a problem may continue to be discussed.

**Skills: posting;
separation of P/I and P/S**

13. The group's enthusiasm may wane after a few problems have been identified. This may result from identifying problems the group feels either cannot or will not be solved. It may come from having spent a lot of energy on defining particular issues or clarifying certain problems. Or the group may be spending its time identifying lots of little problems that no one is very concerned about.

**Skills: prioritizing problems;
jumping to P/S;
identifying motivating
discrepancies**

14. The group members may dismiss all problems by saying "None of these is our fault." Group members may feel that they have little control over anything that goes on. They may feel they should not have control over what goes on. They may be trying to avoid responsibility for problems by blaming other groups or conditions.

**Skills: identifying control over
problems**

Phase 4: Problem Solution

GENERAL OVERVIEW

The activities in the problem-solution phase of the meeting are intended to produce workable, agreed-upon solutions to identified problems that are within the group's control. At the close of this phase, work-group members should be committed to carrying out the specific actions the solutions require, and they should expect to share progress reports at the next meeting.

There are some problems that do not really require a lengthy discussion to arrive at a satisfactory solution. Some problems are relatively unimportant. In such cases, encouraging individual volunteers to take responsibility for an action that will solve the problem may be more efficient, if the group is agreeable, and may actually motivate more concentrated effort on the more difficult problems.

When seeking solutions that require group cooperation, following a specific set of procedures will promote their success. Basically, there are six stages in such a problem-solving discussion: (1) defining the problem, (2) generating solutions, (3) evaluating solutions, (4) selecting a solution, (5) building action steps, and (6) planning for review. It is important that these steps be separated, especially 2 and 3.

Searching for possible solutions is a creative process. Often the first ideas that come to people's minds are not their best ideas. Encouraging group members to present ideas without any immediate evaluation of them, make it likely that more ideas will be offered. One person's idea may spark off an idea for someone else. Holding up this process by evaluating ideas as they are proposed may cause people to forget ideas they have or to withhold ideas, in order to avoid evaluation. The value of and need for every member's contribution should not be forgotten as the group works together to solve its problems.

THINGS THAT *SHOULD* HAPPEN

Stage 1. Defining the problem

1. The problem should be defined to the point where everyone understands its scope and effect. If necessary, specific examples of where the problem has arisen should be given.
2. The importance of the problem should be clarified and communicated to the whole group. Everyone should have a common appreciation of the effect of this problem on how well the group can accomplish its task. Some discussion of how the group might function if this problem were solved is often useful for establishing the proper perspective.
3. The group should try to confirm that the problem they will work on is not merely a symptom of a larger problem they may not have identified. If the underlying cause of the small problem is not identified and dealt with, other small problems may keep appearing.

4. An effort should be made to avoid a situation where particular members become defensive. This stage should merely *define* the problem, not find fault or lay blame. The discussion should stay task-oriented and avoid focusing on personality conflicts.

Stage 2. *Generating solutions*

1. This stage should be clearly defined and separated from other stages. The group should feel free to offer a variety of ideas.

2. The group should understand that no solutions will be evaluated at this stage. Any discussion allowed about a particular idea should be for clarification only. If someone does criticize an idea he should be asked to make an alternative suggestion.

3. When a period of silence ensues, the group should be asked if anyone else has a suggestion. If not, the group should go on to the next phase. The idea-generation phase should not be closed off too soon.

Stage 3. *Evaluating solutions*

1. This stage should also be clearly defined and separated from the previous one. The group should understand that this is the appropriate time to evaluate proposed solutions. This is not to say that no further ideas may be presented. On the contrary, group members should take any opportunity to modify and combine solutions to make them more workable by building on each other's ideas.

2. Ideas should be judged, rather than the people who suggested them. The group should make an effort to separate an idea from its source. Also, group members could support anyone who may personally feel under attack.

3. The group should clarify to some degree the standards it will use for judging solutions such as feasibility or cost. If particular criteria are considered absolute essentials or absolute disqualifiers, everyone should share that perception.

4. The group should try to identify the various positive and negative forces at work in the system that would either help or hinder the solution being proposed. Those forces seen as likely to increase a solution's success should be emphasized and encouraged in order that their full benefit can be obtained.

5. The group should make some effort to look ahead at the potential effects of various solutions. The possible consequences and side-effects of implementing a particular solution should be considered as part of the overall evaluation of that solution.

Stage 4. Selecting a solution

1. After all solutions have been evaluated, the group members should select one that seems to best fit their criteria. If a combination of several originally proposed ideas appears to have merit, that hybrid should be restated as the agreed-upon solution.

2. If the problem by its nature requires a solution in which the group must cooperate for its success, the group's commitment to the selected solution should be tested. The reason for checking out the commitment should be made clear to the group.

3. If time allows, the group should consider an alternative solution. The same criteria for judging should be used, and the second choice should be compared with the first to see which is best.

Stage 5. Building action steps

1. The group should develop a series of action steps to follow in implementing their solution. These steps should be specific and clear to all members of the group.

2. A series of short-term plans for reaching the desired objectives should be very specific with regard to exactly what activities will be undertaken.

3. The action steps to be taken by individual group members should be clearly defined. Any person's individual responsibilities should be clarified and accepted by him.

4. The group should identify the positive and negative forces that might be at work in the system that could affect the progress of the action steps. The group members should have a sense of what they can count on and also what will be against them. This might be a good opportunity to focus on any pertinent strengths that may have been indicated in the group's survey data.

5. A time frame for taking specific action steps should be established. This may prove difficult for later steps in the solution, but group members should have a sense of when the first few steps will be accomplished.

Stage 6. Planning for review

1. The group should share the expectation that progress reports will be made by group members on the action steps taken to implement the group's solution. There should be an understanding that any progress or lack of it should be reported to the whole group.

2. Group members should share the expectation that they will review and re-evaluate any action plans they are carrying out. They should

understand that action plans may need to be modified or stepped up to meet constraints in the system. They should plan to judge the effectiveness of their solutions at future meetings.

3. Specific dates for reporting on at least the first action steps should be set. It should be clear who will report on what steps.

THINGS THAT *MIGHT* HAPPEN

1. The supervisor may evaluate solutions during Stage 2. This evaluation may take several forms. The most obvious is people offering reasons why a particular solution will not work. More subtle forms, which you should discourage just as much, would include cutting off discussion of the solution before it is adequately clarified, joking about a solution, or completely ignoring a proposal.

   Skills: brainstorming

2. Group members may hesitate to offer their ideas for fear of being evaluated. Often people use their own internal criteria, such as feasibility or acceptability, to judge their ideas and do not suggest those that fail their own personal tests.

   Skills: brainstorming

3. Group members may think this whole activity is a waste of time. They may feel that this is a case of "all talk and no action," and that nothing will be done to use the solutions they generate.

   **Info: how group-feedback meeting fits
   in effort**

4. Group members may believe that their superiors are not interested in or really committed to carrying out these activities effectively. They may feel that problems outside their control will never be solved and that efforts they themselves make will be undermined.

   **Skills: identifying control over
   problems**

5. Group members may feel participation is risky. They may feel that their superiors want to use this activity to identify "troublemakers." In the action-planning stage, they may feel that individuals will be held accountable by their superiors for implementing solutions.

   Skills: confidentiality

6. The group may show low energy and commitment at this phase. They may not identify solutions to problems within their control or accept responsibility for planning or carrying out action steps.

   **Skills: identifying motivating
   discrepancies**

Phase 5: Close of the Meeting

GENERAL OVERVIEW

A typical work-group feedback meeting incorporates many different activities into its various phases. It is important that the supervisor take a few minutes at the close of the meeting to summarize what has gone on. He might briefly review whatever agenda items have been covered and the problems that have been worked on and actions that have been planned. This is especially helpful in meetings where there has been a high degree of frustration over identifying problems and solutions by demonstrating to people what they have been able to accomplish despite their conflicts.

To maintain any momentum toward problems solutions that this meeting has generated, some attention should be given to the next group meeting. The supervisor should schedule the next meeting and discuss the next agenda with group members. Reports on action steps decided on in this meeting should be expected at the next meeting. This effort to summarize and schedule is important and should not be neglected, even if time is running short.

After the meeting has ended, the consultant may have a chance to discuss it with the supervisor. You may want to explain certain interventions you made or make suggestions on how the supervisor could handle a particular problem in the future. You might discuss how well the plans made for this meeting worked out and perhaps set a time to discuss the next group meeting.

THINGS THAT *SHOULD* HAPPEN

1. The supervisor should schedule the next session.
2. The group should build an agenda for the next meeting. Items to be discussed should include unfinished business left from this meeting; problems identified as needing solutions, but which the group did not get to; progress reports from the supervisor on problems he has taken to the groups that control them.
3. After the meeting, the consultant should give the supervisor feedback on how he led the meeting. You should make suggestions on how the supervisor might handle problems if they recur, and give specific examples of those problems. You should provide any help he wants on planning for the next meeting.

THINGS THAT *MIGHT* HAPPEN

1. There may have been times during the meeting when the discussion

did not progress well but when, at the same time, it was inappropriate for the consultant to intervene. In situations like this, feedback about the group process might best be given at the close of the meeting.

Skills: giving effective feedback

Section III

Activities and Concepts
at the
Systemic Level

Overview of System-Level Development

This section focuses on the organization as a system of many interdependent people, hierarchical levels, and functional areas. It deals with how to understand, organize, and present survey data and how to identify and solve problems that cut across functional and status lines. Both diagnostic and change activities relevant to development work at the system level are described in detail. The consultant's role in guiding these activities is considered in terms of when interventions are called for and what kinds of interventions are appropriate in various situations.

It is crucial that solutions to problems be based on and generated by a diagnosis of the type, source, scope, and causes of problems in the organization. This means that diagnostic information should be well-prepared and digested, and that diagnosis should *precede* the planning or implementation of any corrective activities. The survey results serve as the diagnostic base, although additional information collected through interviews, observations, or organizational records is often useful.

The ultimate goal of system-level development is to build in the capacity to solve problems that affect overall organization functioning. Making constructive changes in overall organization functioning is crucial to creating a climate in which individual work groups are able to improve their internal functioning, and are motivated to do it. In addition, the problems dealt with at the system level are usually broader in scope than those focused on at the work-group level. Because of the importance and scope of issues dealt with at the system level, active guidance is often required from the consultant to insure that the system problems are dealt with effectively. Therefore, if you are faced with severe time and resource constraints, system-level development should take priority over development activities at the work-group level.

In the event that operating constraints also preclude a complete development effort at the system level, the activities that should receive highest priority are:

- Preparing a systemic diagnosis for organization leaders based on the survey data;
- Presenting the diagnosis to organization leaders;
- Having organization leaders identify some specific problems and their causes, as indicated by the diagnosis; the guidance of a consultant for this activity is necessary in most cases;
- Having organization leaders plan specific action steps to solve at least one identified problem; a consultant should guide this activity.

One note about the format of this manual is merited here: key phrases, e.g., **source of the data**, are used to list examples of interventions the consultant might utilize in various situations. The interventions are described in Module 9 and may be referenced by these key phrases. If you are not familiar with how to locate these descriptions, read the introduction to Module 9 before proceeding with this section.

Module 6
Understanding and Presenting Systemic Data

This module covers concepts and skills you will need to organize and interpret systemic data. The content included here may be divided into two major areas. The first half of the module (Sections 1 to 3) describes the nature and scope of systemic data, focusing on how they are used, the format in which they are reported, and the way they should be organized. The second half of the module (Sections 4 to 6) deals with presenting systemic data. The materials in these sections center on the systemic diagnosis and how it is prepared and presented.

WHAT ARE SYSTEMIC DATA?

The previous three modules have been focusing on work-group data and feedback processes at the group level. Module 3 mentioned that data summarized by individual work group provide the basis for the survey-guided development effort as carried out within each work group. The effort is also carried out at the total system level. For this purpose, an accurate picture is needed of how the whole organization functions, indicating system-wide strengths and weaknesses in a manner similar to the assessment of each work group. Systemic data provide the source from which such a picture is generated. Systemic data group together survey responses from individuals in all work groups throughout the whole organization. Therefore, they are used to focus on functions of the whole system, or cross-sections of it, rather than on individual work groups.

Systemic data may take several forms in addition to summarizing responses of all organization members. For example, responses of all organization members may be broken down by hierarchical level or by functional or departmental area. This means that data from personnel at the same level in the organization hierarchy, or with similar functions, are grouped together. Also, demographic questions from the survey may be used to organize systemic data (e.g., age, sex, level of education, or organization-tenure categories). Regardless of how systemic data re organized or broken down, the goal is to provide a picture of the whole organization's functioning. This picture is further clarified by looking at how the system is perceived by individuals at the same level, with the same function, or from the same length of tenure or age categories, as supplied by the various breakdowns that consultants and system leaders wish to examine.

Systemic data may also be differentiated from work-group data by the target group of system members to whom they are presented. It is clear that work-group data are to be fed back to group members who provided it. In the case of systemic data, however, those who should receive the data are less clearly defined. Systemic data will be most useful to those people who are in a position to guide and influence organization practices, namely, system leaders. These decision-making leaders may include various personnel—uppermost managerial personnel (president, vice presidents, plant manager), department heads, division heads, or a combination of these. Before the data are reported back to the organization, the consultant and the organization member(s) who are in charge of the development project should decide what organization members will receive the data. The decision should consider the ability of the recipients to guide and direct changes in the total system. In addition, a policy on confidentiality of systemic data should be emphasized from the outset of the development effort. Consultants and system leaders decide who should see the data and under what conditions data may be disclosed to individuals or groups other than designated recipients. When such a policy is established, system leaders are assured that the data will not be used by anyone without their knowledge and consent.

ORGANIZING SYSTEMIC DATA

The preliminary aspects of organizing systemic data are much the same as those needed for work-group data. Consequently, if you are thoroughly familiar with the material discussed in Module 3 on understanding work-group data, you are already able to take the first steps in organizing and understanding systemic data. In this section, there is a brief review of the terms involved, including definitions specifically related to systemic data. (See Module 3 for a more complete definition of each of these terms.)

Data Printout

The format in which the data are returned must be clear before any interpretation of the data can be made. The systemic data printout takes much the same form as do work-group data sheets. Therefore, a review of statistical terms provided for each item and index will help you quickly grasp the major features of the data. Refer to Figure 10 and the following corresponding definitions for a brief review of the print-out terms.

1. *Heading.* The title indicates that the data reported are for all organization groups combined. The numerical label gives the same information, showing that all groups with numbers within the specified range have been combined.

2. *Item.* Survey question numbers (or index numbers) and para-phrased item text.

3. *Percentage Distribution.* Percentage of respondents who choose each of the five answer alternatives for each survey question. The percentage distribution indicates the amount of agreement among system members on an item.

4. *Mean.* Average response of system members on a particular item.

5. *Standard deviation.* Like the percentage distribution, the standard deviation measures the amount of agreement among system members by showing how much responses tend to differ from the average or mean response score.

6. *N.* The number of system members responding on any given item.

Standard of Comparison

The notion of the standard of comparison was defined in Module 3, and its importance in measuring *how well* a group or system functions was noted. In order to determine how well a whole organization is functioning, the organization's scores must be compared with scores from all other organizations surveyed. Scores from this larger group of all organizations, or *norms*, may be grouped in several ways: by all organizations combined (total), by levels across organizations, or by functional areas. Therefore, if you use breakdowns of the norms, you can compare like groups from one organization with those from the norms, e.g., first-level organization groups with first-level norm groups. The comparisons you make depend on the types of systemic data groupings that will provide the most meaningful information for the organization and on the available norms. At the least, you need the total norm groups with which any

COMBINED DEPRTS.
GROUPS
1000 TO 2155

ITEM	PERCENTAGE DISTRIBUTION					MEAN	STD DEV.	N
	(1)	(2)	(3)	(4)	(5)			
7 CO USES NEW WK METHODS	2	8	49	30	11	3.40	0.84	329
8 CO INTEREST IN WELFARE	8	20	36	24	12	3.14	1.10	330
9 CO IMPROVES WKING COND	5	13	42	30	9	3.25	0.98	328
10 CO HAS CLEAR GOALS	7	12	35	35	10	3.31	1.04	324
11 WK ACTIVITY ORGANIZED	5	16	43	27	8	3.16	0.97	328
12 YOU GET OTH UNIT INFO	17	27	35	15	5	2.64	1.09	329

Figure 10. Sample system-level data printout

grouping of systemic data may be compared. The actual comparison is made in the manner described in Module 3, where means scores from the organization's data and normative group are compared and a *percentile* score is the result.

Preparation for Systemic Data Analysis

The role of the consultant in analyzing systemic data breaks down into two essential tasks or phases. As you work with the data, differences between these two phases may be more implicit than explicit, but it is important that you are aware of them, because they influence your approach to the data. The first task may be called the analysis phase. During this phase, your aim is to gain a thorough and comprehensive understanding of how the system functions as evidenced in the data. The way you work through the data for your own understanding does not necessarily correspond point-by-point with the way you organize the data for presenting them to system leaders, however. This latter task suggests that the second phase of your role could be called the feedback-strategy phase. For this task, your aim is to prepare to present the data so that they mobilize system leaders' energy to work on important problem areas shown in the data. These two phases overlap to some extent: both require familiarization with major strengths and weaknesses and with important areas of system functioning as described by the data. In the first phase, you draw upon all the data to formulate an objective and detailed picture of what the data show. Based on this formulation, the second phase involves focusing the data in a workable manner so that they are accessible to organization leaders. The material immediately following covers activities undertaken mainly during the analysis phase. Section 4-C, toward the end of this module, deals more extensively with the strategy issues you should consider as you prepare the data for feedback to system leaders.

CAUSAL FLOW OF EVENTS

Once you have obtained percentile scores for various systemic data runs, you need some basis for deciding how index scores are related, or how they influence each other. The causal flow of events shows how various aspects of organizational functioning are related. Module 3 examines this sequence as it applies to interpreting work-group level data. This section describes the operation of this sequence at a system-wide level.

    In looking at the functioning of a whole organization, we may describe it as a system made up of many interrelated parts: levels, functions, groups, individuals. The basic building block of the organization is the face-to-face work group or team, consisting of the supervisor and those subordinates who report directly to him. The work group is considered a building block because it is the setting for major work-related interactions. Each group's supervisor links his group of subordinates to upper level groups in two ways. First, he transmits the policies and information originating from upper levels down to his subordinates, and he transmits information and expression of feelings from his subordinates up to higher level personnel. He does this by sharing information and ideas in his own peer group and through interaction processes at the next higher level. This suggests the second aspect of the supervisor's linking position. His dual role means he is a supervisor of one group, and a subordinate in his peer group at the immediate higher level in the organization. This is illustrated in Figure 11, using by-level breakdowns that represent one way of grouping systemic data into hierarchical sections. All groups in the organization are linked by way of the supervisor's dual role.

The supervisor's linking function aids understanding of how parts of the system fit together as a coherent, interacting whole. This structural frame of reference allows one to examine the causal sequence of key factors that describe the functioning of the system. As measured by the Survey of Organizations, these factors include: organizational climate, supervisory leadership, peer leadership, group process, and satisfaction. The system-wide flow of these factors describes relationships between behaviors in groups at one level and behaviors in groups above or below that level in the hierarchy, as shown in Figure 12. By the scope of their authority and responsibility, groups at the top (those supervised by the president, vice-president, and division managers) have a greater effect on conditions within which groups nearer the bottom must work than do lower level groups.

For example, first-line supervisors and their subordinates have less latitude in their behavior and in setting policies than do division managers and their subordinates. Higher level groups produce outputs of policies, objectives, and decisions that influence the atmosphere in which work activities at subsequent levels are carried out, or *organizational climate*. Climate conditions for any work group are largely shaped by the group processes of those groups above it in the hierarchy. Thus, climate is experienced differently by groups at different levels, since outputs of policies and procedures from groups accumulate and practices become increasingly constraining further down the hierarchy. Since practices and job activities in each work group are carried out within the bounds of climate conditions transmitted from higher levels, organizational climate is designated as the primary causal factor

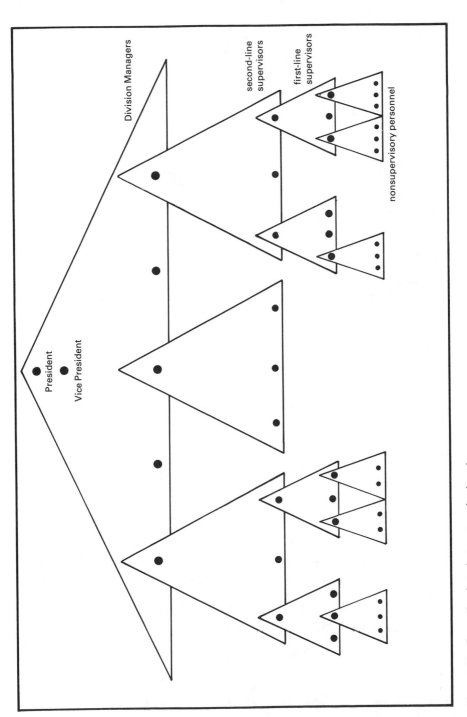

Figure 11. Organizational structure by level

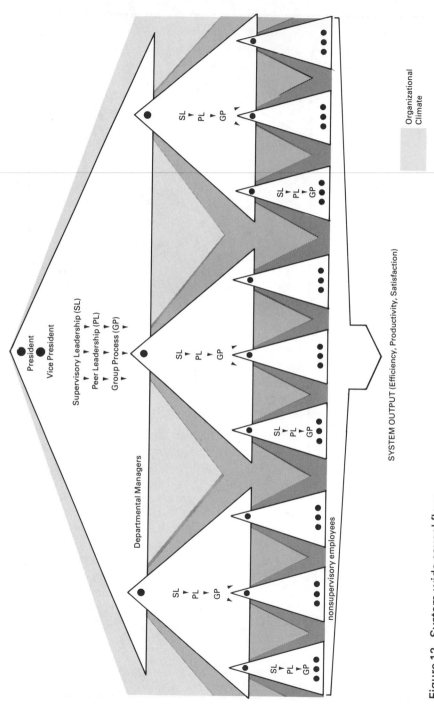

Figure 12. System-wide causal flow

in the causal flow of events. Specifically, the climate conditions include the decision-making practices, communication flow, motivational conditions, human-resources primacy, lower level influence, and technological readiness indices on the Survey of Organizations.

Because of the constraints that organizational climate produces, supervisors have varying degrees of control over their own leadership practices. The amount of control they have is largely dependent on their position in the hierarchy, and their influence in setting organizational policies and procedures. For example, whether supervisors help subordinates to solve job problems or to plan work ahead (measured on the Survey of Organizations by the supervisory work facilitation index) reflects the extent to which supervisors receive enough information from upper levels about work objectives or have inputs to decisions made (measured by the climate indices of decision-making practices and communication flow).

While supervisory leadership practices partially reflect the organizational climate in which leadership is carried out, supervisory leadership itself influences other factors. Within each work group, a supervisor acts in ways that affect behaviors among his subordinates toward each other. In providing such a model, supervisory-leadership strengths and weaknesses influence peer-leadership behavior. Peer leadership, in turn, determines the smoothness and effectiveness of work-group interactions and teamwork as measured by the group-process index. Satisfaction of organization members is a final outcome resulting in large measure from the effectiveness of work-team interactions and organizational policies in meeting individuals' needs.

As shown in Figure 12, the causal flow takes place within groups at each level, and in so doing, produces outputs that influence groups at levels immediately following in the systemic hierarchy. Specifically, outputs from group process at one level affect subsequent levels' experience of organizational climate. In other words, the interactions of a supervisor within his peer group (as described by group process) determines the situation (organization climate) in which the group he supervises must operate. As mentioned above, work groups at each level are exposed to different influence from above, so descriptions of organizational climate will vary at each level. The causal flow thus operates within levels, and from level to level as well. Having this system-wide causal flow in mind, then, one can look for patterns of influence indicated in by-level systemic data. This causal flow should become more meaningful to you as you apply it in describing concrete situations shown by the data.

ANALYZING THE DATA: SYSTEMIC DIAGNOSIS

What is a systemic diagnosis?

Primarily, a systemic diagnosis is a *description* of what summarized data from all organization members show. A diagnosis is *not* a criticism of the way the organization is run or a list of laid-on solutions as to what should be happening. In describing the present state of the organization, the diagnosis emphasizes the strengths as well as the weaknesses shown by the data. All information provided in the diagnosis should be tied directly to evidence from the survey data provided by organization members.

The diagnosis is prepared and presented by the consultant to top-level system leaders. It may also be disseminated (in total or in summarized form) to additional organization members at other echelons. Its dissemination should comply with the previously-made decision as to who should see the systemic data (i.e., confidentiality of systemic data). The diagnosis is used by the consultant and organization leaders as a basis for deciding where in the organization changes are needed and what changes can and should be made.

The diagnostic description of major systemic strengths and weaknesses uses at least two approaches to the data. First, systemic data may be broken down by hierarchical level. One way systemic data may be grouped by level, as illustrated earlier in this module, is the following:

1. Top level: summarized data from all individuals in the organization who report directly to the president and vice president.

2. Second level: summarized data from all individuals who report directly to division managers.

3. Third level: summarized data from all individuals who report directly to second-line supervisors.

4. Lowest level: summarized data from all individuals who report directly to first-line supervisors.

Data for each of these levels, and any additional intermediate levels that may be needed to describe a particular organizational hierarchy, are described in terms of major strengths and weaknesses. By-level descriptions provide specific information about where various problems are located in the organization hierarchy.

Second, the data that are summarized over all levels, or total organization data, are examined. Used together, these two ways of summarizing systemic data—by level and total—provide both a general picture of the organization's functioning and specific information about functions at each level that make up the total. As you may realize, the levels with the most people, that is, the lower echelons, will have the greatest influence on total organization data.

Thus, the diagnosis indicates where in the organization the problem areas have varying degrees of impact. Scores on one index at different levels indicate the prevalence or extent of strength or weakness in that area across levels. Given information about where problems are reported, organization leaders have a realistic notion of how the system functions and of problems that affect the whole organization's effectiveness.

However, in order to take steps to lessen problems, one needs to find the source(s) and, if possible, the cause(s) of such problems. Using the data and the theory underlying the survey, the diagnosis suggests where to look for possible causes or origins of particular problems. On the basis of relationships among items and indices, the diagnosis explores additional evidence that a suspected problem is, in fact, present. By focusing on related items, supporting or refuting information is obtained about suspected problem areas. (See Module 2 to review indices and the use of non-index items.) Ways in which items and indices are related and examples of how to get this additional evidence were provided as a part of the causal flow of events discussion earlier in the module.

Data-based statements seek to determine possible origins of problem areas by describing (1) relationships among indices and items, (2) influences from level to level within the organization. In investigating these relationships, the diagnosis may also suggest instances where additional information is needed to pinpoint causal factors.

Interpreting Systemic Data

The material provided in this section demands a solid grasp of all areas that have been mentioned in this module. The three main concepts around which the following discussion is organized should be reviewed:

1. *Organizational level:* refers to a cross-sectional grouping of organization personnel who occupy like positions in the hierarchical chain of command (see Module 6, Sections 3 and 4-A). Systemic data may be summarized by *level*.

2. *Unit of data:* data are reported in two units: (a) by a single questionnaire item and (b) by index, which is an average of responses over several survey items describing a particular behavior or area of functioning. Remember, not all survey items are clustered to form indices. Indices, in turn may be grouped to describe a larger domain

of functioning, i.e., organizational climate, supervisory leadership, peer leadership (see Module 2 and Module 6, Section 2).

3. *Level of score:* refers to the percentile score that measures how well an organization or organization level is doing on a particular item or index compared with the norms. Percentile scores may fall within a high, average, or low range and indicate strong or weak areas of functioning (see Module 3, "Standard of Comparison," and Module 6, Section 2).

Assume that you have received the organization's data—both total and by-level breakdowns—and have computed percentile scores using the appropriate norms. You are also familiar with the way indices are related according to the system-wide causal flow of events. Now you are ready to begin looking at what the data show and to examine various possibilities as to why the behaviors described by the data are present.

Examining the data for the total organization is a useful place to start since doing so provides a general perspective for later detailed analysis. Begin by sorting out index scores into high, low, and average percentile score categories. As mentioned in Module 3, scores within the 40-60th percentile range are generally considered as average. To the extent that scores are above or below this range, strong or weak areas are suggested. The causal flow indicates that you should look at indices and items that comprise the organizational climate area first. Problem areas and strong points among climate indices will suggest conditions that may hamper or facilitate leadership practices and the task performance of organization members. Look for clusters of climate indices—are scores generally high, low, average, or mixed? If scores are mixed, what are highest and lowest areas, and how great is the spread of scores? What motivating discrepancies do the data show?

Once you have identified strengths and weaknesses in organizational climate, you use the same strategy to see what is happening in leadership and group process areas. In other words, your purpose is to learn the extent and nature of the causal flow as reflected in the organization's data. In the process of identifying high, average, and low-scoring areas and tracing the causal sequence, you may also look at the affect these four aspects of organizational functioning—climate, supervisory leadership, peer leadership and group process—are having on various end-result measures. On the Survey of Organizations, items within the satisfaction index represent such measures.

As a part of the sorting-out process, you should look not only at index scores, but also at the items that make up the indices. The item scores allow you to further zero in on possible problem areas, or uncover problems that the more general index score may mask. The main question is whether item scores are clustered together or whether there is a great difference in scores among index items. For example, suppose you find that the score on the communication flow index is at the 40th percentile. The items that make up the index have the following percentile scores: item 12, 55th percentile; item 13, 37th percentile; item 14, 35th percentile. In this example, the index score gives only a general indication that a communication problem may exist. Item scores show that downward communication (item 13) and upward communication (item 14) are seen by organization members as weaker than lateral communication (item 12).

Worksheets similar to that shown in Figure 13 may be used to help you organize the indices and items by providing a ready reference of scores. You should arrange the indices in the order they are to be considered, using the causal sequence as a guide. You may have one set of worksheets for the total organization and a set for each level within the organization.

Organizing scores for the combined responses over the total organization is a useful starting point for two reasons. First, you obtain a general idea of how the system as a whole is functioning. Second, you can practice applying the causal flow in interpreting scores for the total, in preparation for the more complex task of tracing the influence of causal relationships across levels.

Remember, however, that the information you gain in examining combined scores is limited by its general nature. It is important, therefore, that you avoid making hard-and-fast conclusions at this point. Because all individuals at all levels and in all departments are grouped together, total scores mask more specific information about how parts of the organization function, which determine the effectiveness of the total organization. Therefore, unless you are working with a very small organization, or a unit that cannot be meaningfully broken down into levels, you will obtain the most useful diagnostic information by examining each level and making comparisons across levels.

The more specific you can be with regard to particular problem areas, the level of their greatest impact and probable source, the more useful the diagnosis in enabling system leaders to translate the information into concrete practices and conditions. The point to be stressed here is that the total scores may be helpful to you as an overview or starting point, but may be detrimental if over-used in the diagnosis itself. The by-level data and cross-level comparisons give the kind of information that can be more readily used by system leaders.

Having organized the scores and obtained a general idea of how the organization as a whole is functioning, the next step is to go through the same process at each level within the organization. In doing this, you

CLIMATE	MEAN	PERCENTILE SCORE
Decision-Making Practices Index	_____	_____
31—Objectives set jointly	_____	_____
32—Decision levels optimum	_____	_____
33—Decision-makers seek ideas	_____	_____
34—Decision-makers get information	_____	_____
Communication-Flow Index		
12—U get other unit information	_____	_____
13—Supervisors open to ideas	_____	_____
14—Told enough to do job	_____	_____
Motivational-Conditions Index		
15—Disagreements worked thru	_____	_____
23—Motivation to work hard	_____	_____
25—Conditions encourage hard work	_____	_____
Human-Resources-Primacy Index		
8—Co interest in welfare	_____	_____
9—Co improves work conditions	_____	_____
11—Work activities organized	_____	_____
Lower-Level-Influence Index		
27—Influence first level on department	_____	_____
29—Influence employee on department	_____	_____
Technological-Readiness Index		
7—Co uses new work method	_____	_____
99—Equipment adequate	_____	_____
SUPERVISORY LEADERSHIP		
Goal-Emphasis Index		
42—Supervisor encourages effort	_____	_____
44—Supervisor has high standards	_____	_____
Work-Facilitation Index		
46—Supervisor shows how to improve	_____	_____
48—Supervisor helps plan ahead	_____	_____
50—Supervisor offers new ideas	_____	_____

Figure 13. Sample display reference sheet

may note how scores at each level contribute to or deviate from patterns in the total organization data that you have tentatively drawn. Since the flow of influence in the system generally moves from the top down to lower echelons, you may look at levels in that order. Your purpose is to examine what conditions or behaviors (described by index scores as strong or weak) at the top level are influencing the next level (by comparing reported strengths and weaknesses) and so on. As you move down the hierarchy, your goal is to arrive at various interacting patterns of climate conditions, leadership, and group process by sorting out high and low areas at each level, and comparing scores across levels.

Once you are able to describe what the data show at each level, your task is to look for possible reasons *why* levels show various strengths and weaknesses and where problems may be originating. In order to do this you need to look at specific aspects of the data from a level-to-level perspective. For example, you can trace leadership indices from top to bottom levels to see what differences or similarities supervisors at each level are described as having by their subordinates. Questions to ask in this process include: Are there problems that seem prevalent at one level and no other? Do practices at one level influence problems at lower levels? Are task-related leadership indices (goal emphasis and work facilitation) generally stronger or weaker than interpersonal areas (support and team building) or are scores mixed in these areas? How do trends in supervisory leadership affect trends in peer leadership, both within and across levels?

In trying to discover patterns on any index or area of functioning, you must remember that any problem area is a result of many factors working together. For example, suppose you find that supervisory support and work facilitation are low at the middle level in the organization. Supervisors may be constrained by the climate situation, particularly by decision making or communication flow, so check scores on these indices. However, supervisors' values, personality factors, or lack of skills or knowledge may also inhibit their effectiveness in these areas. You may need more information than the survey items to really define why a problem in any area exists. However, the causal flow gives you a basis to start your search for problem sources.

For another example, suppose you are tracing climate indices down through the levels, and all levels are average except the lowest level. Organizational climate, as experienced by the lowest level, is largely a result of things that are going on at the next highest level in the organization. The group behaviors at that higher level included in the group process index—group planning and coordination, information sharing, decision making and problem solving—lead to outputs of policies, practices, and procedures from that level. The quality and efficiency of those outputs are only as good as the *process* involved in making them. These outputs directly impinge on lower level groups and their supervisors by shaping the latitudes and constraints they have in fulfilling their roles and tasks. Therefore, when lower level groups report on climate conditions, it is the outputs from the next higher level that are being described. If the group process index at that higher level is weak, the outputs produced will also suffer, and so the climate experienced at the subsequent level is accordingly expected to show weaknesses. Consequently, when climate at one level is low, look to see what aspects of group process at the next highest level may be producing constraints in the form of climate conditions at the lower level.

Some further examples for interpreting the data are these:

- Are top-level characteristics being passed down and multiplied at lower levels?

(Example: Climate scores show a consistent increasing or decreasing trend with movement down the hierarchy.)

- Are there task-related or interpersonal problems that are felt at some levels more than others?

(Your additional knowledge of the organization may be helpful in this case. Perhaps supervisors at one level have interpersonal conflicts among themselves; perhaps the supervisor's role at a particular level is by definition a difficult "middle-man" role; perhaps work-load pressures are directly felt at some levels more than at others by the nature of the work and scheduling demands, etc.)

- Are supervisors at one level acting as buffers for their subordinates, or protecting them from poor climate conditions existing higher up?

(Example: Look for relatively high scores in climate areas at lower levels as compared to lower climate scores at higher levels in the organization.)

- Are certain organization policies hindering practices at certain levels more than others and why?

(Levels at which the product of the organization is actually produced, i.e., lowest levels, may be most greatly affected by blockage in communication flow or failure of higher level personnel to plan ahead and organize work activities sensibly. A poor climate passed down through the hierarchy may hinder job satisfaction and productivity to the greatest extent at lower levels.)

- Do all levels feel they have inputs to organization policies and practices?

(Check decision-making items at all levels, also communication flow items to see where differences exist as perceived by organization members at these levels.)

- Where is more information needed on the source(s) of problems?

(Differentiate between where a problem impacts and where it may originate. Often, you can only hypothesize various sources using evidence from the data. Sometimes a problem area may seem isolated from any substantiating evidence, and you may need information other than survey data to explain its source. If the problem seems to be an important one, you may wish to get more information yourself, or recommend ways to obtain it. Organization leaders need to know sources if possible, to begin to alleviate problems effectively in the right area.)

In interpreting the data, you should be careful to check your assumptions with all of the supporting data you can find. Anything you report in the diagnosis should be carefully and fully documented by what the data show. As suggested above, look at the data from as many perspectives as you can in describing what patterns of influence are reflected. Do not try to be too specific without supporting data, but at the same time, remember that loose generalities will be useless.

The guidelines outlined in this section for making a diagnostic interpretation of systemic data may be briefly summarized as follows:

1. Organize total organization data. Look for strong and weak points among indices and items within each major area of the causal sequence. Try to discover relationships among scores from different indices.

2. Organize data at each organization level. Begin with the top level and move down the hierarchy citing strong and weak points at each level.

3. Compare data across levels. Focus on how the causal flow influences conditions at each level and how scores at one level may be affecting conditions at subsequent levels. Note features that are distinct at one or two levels and those that are common to all levels.

4. Look for possible reasons why conditions exist at each level. Distinguish between where problems make their impact and where (at what level and in what behavioral or functional area) they may be originating. Where a problem area seems evident, look at related indices and items to further clarify and confirm the extent and nature of the problem.

5. Make sure all your descriptive statements are based on the data and that you have taken all relevant data into account in making them.

Realize that you may need additional information to define a problem area, and that your goal is to highlight areas that can be profitably tackled by system leaders.

STRATEGY ISSUES IN PREPARING THE DIAGNOSIS

Up to this point, consideration has been given to activities involved in analyzing the data that result in the content of the systemic diagnosis. In preparing the diagnosis, you will also be aware of the particular organization leaders who will be receiving the data you are analyzing. This means you will be constantly asking yourself various questions that, in addition to characteristics of the data themselves, will also influence the way you prepare and present the diagnosis. These questions are strategy issues, to be answered in ways that maximize the usefulness and motivating impact of the data for organization leaders. Examples of such questions include:

- With what aspects of the data should you begin?
- In what order should you move through the data?
- How much data should be presented?
- What strengths should be capitalized on?
- What problems should be emphasized?
- What aspects of the data will be motivating for this particular organization at this present time?
- Should a model of systemic functioning be used in presenting the data? Which one?
- What graphics might be useful?

Other questions of this type will occur to you as you prepare the diagnosis. Also, important considerations that require your exploration should come to mind as you seek to answer these kinds of questions. Examples of these considerations include:

- System leaders' background, receptivity, sharpness;
- Organization members' attitudes toward surveys, toward numbers, toward the survey-guided-development effort;
- Expectations of system leaders about what the data will indicate;
- Organization's operating schedule, time constraints;
- Present motivation of organization members to work for a constructive change;
- Quality of data set (high, low, or average overall score level);

- Clarity of causal model as shown in data;
- Consultant time, or number of consultants available to help with feedback.

The characteristics of considerations like these listed will be used to answer the strategy questions that in your judgment will make a crucial difference in whether system leaders accept and utilize their data as a tool for planning and implementing actions that will promote productive change in the organization's functioning. The diagnosis and the way it is presented will be most helpful to system leaders to the extent that it highlights areas that need strengthening and that can be profitably worked on. These are strategies you must consider in preparing the systemic diagnosis before presenting systemic data in feedback meetings. Specific strategies for guiding feedback meetings will be examined in Modules 7 and 8.

PREPARING FOR THE PRESENTATION

There are several considerations that you must bear in mind as you prepare to present the diagnostic information you have gathered. First, the diagnosis may be presented either by written report or by verbal presentation. If the latter form is chosen, it will be helpful before your presentation if you distribute a brief summary of what the data show to system leaders so that they have some notion of the major areas you have focused on.

Second, regardless of the form in which you present the data, your prime concern should be the level of preparation that system leaders have regarding systemic data. Remember, system leaders are not experienced in working with the data and may have only a vague idea of how you have organized the data or how they may be interpreted and used.

One way to prepare system leaders for receiving systemic data is to arrange a session to familiarize them with some of the basic aspects of the data: how the survey is used and organized, what systemic data look like, how percentile scores are generated, how indices are related, and so forth. If such an opportunity is not available, you may wish to compile some written explanatory material. This would be distributed to system leaders before they receive the data and might be devised along the lines of a feedback package at the systemic level. (See Module 3 for details on the work-group feedback package.)

At any rate, when you present the diagnosis, you must realize that many of the concepts and terms involved will be relatively new to system leaders and should be explicitly, yet simply, explained as part of the diagnostic presentation.

As you prepare the diagnosis, several essentials should be included:

- A brief theoretical introduction that covers:

  The concept of the organization as a system made up of work teams linked together by the supervisor;

  What the survey measures;

  The meaning of survey indices and their causal relationship.

- A definition of the norms to which the organization's data were compared, what a percentile score means, and how high, average and low scores are determined;

- An explanation of how the data have been summarized and which organization members are included in each level;

- Charts that illustrate the major features of the data and highlight relationships among indices and levels (see Figures 14 and 15 for examples);

- Suggestions for how the information contained in the diagnosis may be used.

By this time, you no doubt realize that there is a great deal of information that must be presented to system leaders and understood by them. Therefore, the more time you are able to spend in examining the data yourself, and in presenting the data to system leaders, the more useful the information will be as a tool for increasing the effectiveness of the organization. The way in which you organize the data to highlight motivating discrepancies is the key for the usefulness of the survey information for the total organization.

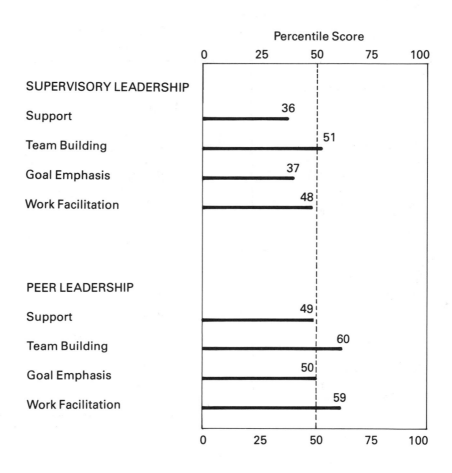

Figure 14. Leadership indices

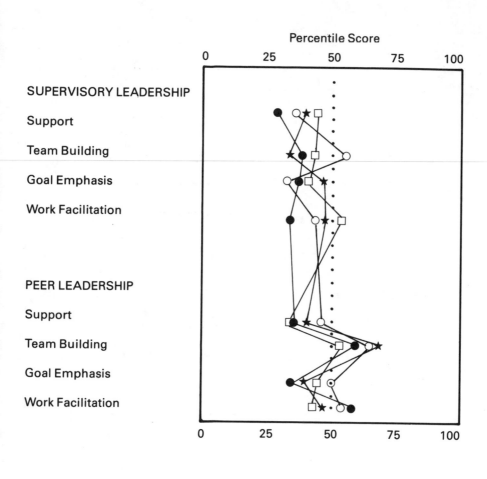

Figure 15. Leadership indices—cross-level comparison

Module 7
Identifying Systemic Problems

SYSTEMIC PROBLEMS

A problem in organizational functioning is defined as the presence or absence of specific behaviors, policies, or conditions that interfere with the effective functioning of an organization. As was stated in Module 1, it is crucial that problems in organizational functioning be defined accurately if effective solutions are to be planned and carried out. In survey-guided development, a problem area is indicated by discrepancies between how the organization actually functions, as indicated by people who fill out the standardized survey, and the ideal level of functioning, set by some standard of comparison. (See Modules 1 and 3 for a review of the standard of comparison notion.)

The seriousness of a problem depends on at least two factors. First, it depends on the *size of the discrepancy* between actual and ideal functioning. For example, if survey norms are being used as the ideal standard of comparison for an organization or unit, a percentile score of 20 on communication flow would indicate a more serious problem than a percentile score of 45. Percentile scores of 30 on communication flow and 50 on decision making would indicate that the more serious problem lies in communication flow.

Second, the seriousness of a problem area depends on the *importance* of the aspect or dimension of organizational functioning. The position of an area of functioning in the causal model of organizational behavior, its relationship to valued organizational outcomes, and people's level of concern about any one aspect of functioning—all determine the importance of a problem area. Therefore, a low percentile score in any given aspect of organizational functioning is most serious when it (a) affects other crucial aspects of the human organization, (b) affects the quality or quantity of products or services produced, and/or (c) generates the concern of many people in the organization.

What are Systemic Problems?

Viewing an organization as a "system" necessitates the consideration of behaviors and working relationships of many people in many jobs and roles, at various hierarchical levels in the organization, under varying internal and external conditions, and at many points in time. Thus, when one is interested in identifying systemic problems, the focus should be on:

1. Organizational problems common to many people in many roles at various hierarchical levels for some period of time (that is, the same problems in the same form for many people); or

2. Organizational problems found in *one* form in some groups of people, which in turn create problems of *another* form for other groups; or

3. Organizational problems found exclusively in one or a few groups, but where those groups or their problems are so crucial to the functioning of the organization that their problems may be considered problems for the whole organization.

A few examples may help to clarify what these three types of systemic problems look like:

Assume that you have a computer printout that shows the survey results for three hierarchical levels in an organization: top-management level, middle management or department-head level, and first-line supervision level.

• Example 1: *Systemic problem of same form for many people*.

The diagnosis indicates that at all levels the scores on peer team building are the lowest. They are at or below the 30th percentile for all three echelons. A systemic problem is indicated in this area. People do not know how to, are not willing to, or do not have the opportunity to work together as a team.

• Example 2: *Systemic problem of changing form*.

The diagnosis indicates that the lowest score at the top level is on peer team building, at the middle-management level is on communication flow, and at the first-line level is on supervisory goal emphasis. The percentile scores on these indices are all below average. A systemic problem like the following may be indicated: Although the departmental managers have a satisfactory working relationship with top-level managers, they do not work together as a team (indicated by the low percentile scores on peer building). This means that a departmental manager may not get needed information about what the work schedules, goals, and deadlines are for departments other than his own. At the departmental management level, this lack of information may create a climate problem in the area of communication flow. The people reporting to the department heads (i.e., first-line supervisors) may find that schedules or goals are often changed in midstream or are not set at all because information about other departments' schedules is not communicated to their department head. At the first-line supervisory level, this might result in poor supervisory goal emphasis on their part; that is, a first-line supervisor may not be able to set goals and schedule work ahead of time for his subordinates because department goals are subject to change depending on when his department head finds out what other related departments are doing. This is a case where poor teamwork at the top level of the organization undermines communication at the middle level, which in turn results in low supervisory goal emphasis at the lower level.

• Example 3: *An isolated systemic problem.*
The diagnosis indicates that a few work groups report extremely low job challenge and little satisfaction with jobs. Additional information from interviews and company records indicate that both the turnover and accident rates in these units are particularly high. Although the number of groups reporting this may be few, the problems suggested in safety conditions or incentive systems may have system-wide ramifications and may require investigation at the systemic level.

As the examples illustrate, systemic problems may take a variety of forms. Basically, however, they are problems for the whole organization, as opposed to a particular work group, and as such they cut across functions, echelons, indices, and time. They indicate what conditions, policies, or behaviors in one part of the organization create problems for other parts of the organization—that is, they reflect complex cause and effect relationships.

The Causes of Systemic Problems

As stated previously, a critical step in organizational development is to identify systemic problems. Problems in organizational functioning are indicated by the systemic diagnosis. However, the causes of these problems must also be explored before a clear statement of problems can be made. This book proposes that problems are caused by deficiencies in one or more of four areas: (1) information, (2) skills, (3) values, or (4) the situation in which individuals and groups work. Deficiencies in the first three of these areas may be evaluated in terms of individual members of the organization. Situation is a more general area relevant to groups and major sub-units of the organization. The strengths and weaknesses in these four areas determine the size and nature of problems that will be found in the system. [1]

INFORMATION

People's behavior depends to some extent on the information—including perceptions and expectations—they have acquired over time regarding what is effective or appropriate behavior. Insufficient or inaccurate information about the technical aspects of a job results in mis-used and damaged equipment, as well as in accidents and inefficiency. Similarly, inadequate information about how people should be organized and managed results in inefficient use of human resources. Invalid models of organizational functioning based on incomplete or mistaken notions about what makes an organization effective can lead to widespread and severe negative consequences for the organization. For example, a manager who knows nothing about the notion of teamwork cannot be expected to encourage his subordinates to work as a team, although worker cooperation might increase the effectiveness of his unit.

SKILLS

Lack of skills related to technical and interpersonal aspects of work is another cause of problems in organizational functioning. One may speak of a person's ability or inability to operate a piece of machinery or design an accounting system as being dependent on his technical skills. Important social skills include those that influence the way in which people interact and work together. These often are referred to as leadership and group-process skills.

The distinction between technical and social skills and the importance of social skills for organizational success frequently seem to be ignored. People often assume that technical skills are more important than social skills for accomplishing organizational goals. A second assumption is that technical skills require special training, while skills in organizing and supervising people can be picked up along the way.

---

[1]This section draws heavily on material from a previous report, "Matching Problems, Precursors, and Interventions in OD: A Systemic Approach," by David G. Bowers, Jerome L. Franklin, and Patricia A. Pecorella. Published in *The Journal of Applied Behavioral Science*, 1975, 11(4), 391-409. Copyright 1975 by NTL Institute for Applied Behavioral Science. Used by permission.

Because of these assumptions, technical training in organizations is more greatly emphasized than training in interpersonal skills.

One clear indication of these assumptions is the promotion of people to managerial positions on the basis of their technical abilities. Such promotions are often made with little training in management concepts—often only a brief review of the organization's official managerial policies is provided. This practice reflects and reinforces the idea that managers' social skills are not terribly important and may be learned simply by being a manager.

Still another common assumption is that social skills cannot really be taught—people are either naturally skillful or not in this area.

The experiences and observations gathered through much research show that these somewhat conflicting assumptions—concerning the relative unimportance of social skills, the ease of attaining social skills, and the nontrainable nature of these skills—are all ill-founded.

VALUES

Every individual carries a set of values or beliefs that influence his or her behavior. When an individual's basic values foster behavior that leads to ineffective organizational functioning, the consequences for the organization will be harmful. For example, a supervisor may believe that people are unimportant and replaceable resources compared to the physical facilities and equipment, despite the fact that without competent, motivated people who want to stay with the organization, the equipment cannot be operated. Such a supervisor values physical resources above human resources and this is bound to be reflected in the way he treats subordinates.

SITUATION

Individuals and groups do not operate independently of each other in organizations. Nor is behavior independent of the physical setting and technological requirements of the job. As was the case in the consideration of information and skills, the situation can be evaluated in terms of both technical and social aspects. Machines and standardized procedures (i.e., accounting systems, etc.) determine which tasks are to be performed and in what order.

Like technology, the structure of the organization has tremendous influence over individual and group behaviors within an organization. Structure greatly determines the patterns of work-related and social relationships found in organizations. Individuals who at about the same hierarchical level work in close physical proximity are likely to interact more and be more friendly than are those at different hierarchical levels who do not see each other often. Consequently, there often are high degrees of camaraderie among members of the same group or department and some distrust between members of different groups or departments.

Aspects of the situation also include less well-recognized factors such as organizational climate. The following examples illustrate how the behavior of each organization member is partially determined by the combined influences of these factors. A situation might exist in which a supervisor is greatly constrained in his leadership behaviors by the organizational climate. If the organization's policies discourage the holding of group meetings, this will inhibit the supervisor's ability to promote teamwork among his subordinates. Consequently, the subordinates will be less able to work together as a team, although such teamwork would be helpful on the job.

Another example of the effects of these situational factors on the behavior of organization members is in the standards of performance established by a supervisor. A situation in which objectives are unreasonable, unattainable, or unclear hinders the supervisor's ability to maintain high standards of performance. In such a situation the supervisor must devote more time to defending the objectives than to facilitating his subordinates' attempts to attain the objectives.

In summary, problems may be caused by a lack of information or skills, conflicting values, or a situation that does not allow people to behave effectively. When system leaders define systemic problems, the consultant should encourage them to find out which of these four factors are the cause(s) of the problem. Also, the system leaders should find out where deficiencies in these areas originate in the organization and who is affected by them.

PROBLEM IDENTIFICATION AT THE SYSTEM LEVEL

A note about format: in the following pages, six kinds of information are given. First, there are some general notes about systemic problem identification and how it differs from identifying problems at the work-group level.

After this general information, there is a list of events that should occur during a meeting held to identify systemic problems. You might consider these as guidelines for a good session. If they do not occur, the consultant should try to judge whether the activities that are occurring are appropriate, given the objectives of the session. If they are not, you should be prepared to step in and guide the meeting in the appropriate direction.

Then, a second set of events is listed; namely, those things that might occur during a problem-identification session and that need to be dealt with if they do. You might consider these problems that should be avoided in a good meeting. If these things happen, the consultant should once again step in and provide the necessary information or use the necessary skills to keep the meeting in a more productive vein. After each such item, one or more key phrases are listed (e.g., **causal model; dealing with resistance**). These key phrases refer to the techniques, that is, the information and skills that the consultant might use in the situation described. These techniques are defined and illustrated in Module 9 and can be referenced by their key phrases.

Fourth, a procedural option is described regarding when systemic problem identification might take place in a full survey-guided development effort.

Fifth, some mechanisms are suggested that might enable organization leaders to hold these sessions in the event that a consultant is not available to guide the process.

Finally, the major issues addressed in this module are highlighted by a listing of key points.

GENERAL OVERVIEW

Ideally, before this phase of the effort begins, the consultant will have presented the systemic diagnosis to organization leaders. The systemic diagnosis indicates the *areas* in which there are problems and the *kinds* of problems that exist. At this point the system leaders and the consultant meet to identify specific problems, their causes, and the order in which they should be addressed. The person who has primary responsibility for leading the meeting is less clearly indicated than is the case for a work-group meeting on problem-solving, where the work-group supervisor is the leader. At the systemic level, the meeting may be led by a top manager (i.e., president, vice president, plant manager), by an organization member who is the designated coordinator of the development effort, or by the consultant himself. In any case, the consultant will assume a more active role in the systemic meeting than in the work-group meeting, as a source of guidance and information. Some preparation and planning for the meeting should be done by the consultant together with the organization member(s) in charge of the meeting. The active involvement of system leaders in the meeting is crucial because system problems are within the control of the top-level group more than any other group in the organization.

The focus of the meeting(s) is the organization's tasks and related information and problems, using the systemic diagnosis as a basis for discussion. The participants may decide that more information should be gathered before the problems can be specifically defined and their causes clearly understood. However, the diagnosis is used as a tool for highlighting the areas needing attention.

The problems identified are systemic; that is, they are problems affecting the whole organization. Because of the systemic focus, the problems identified at meetings such as this are likely to be of a different scope or level than those identified at the work-group level. Whereas a work group might identify something like conflicting demands from the supervisor as a problem, the system leaders might define lack of clarity about the priority of goals as a problem. This does not mean, however, that problems identified at the work-group level are irrelevant to system leaders. Rather, information about work-group problems, when consolidated appropriately, adds more detail to the systemic diagnosis and may help system leaders to formulate more accurately the systemic problems facing the organization.

The steps involved in the problem-identification process at the system level are very similar to those involved at the work-group level. (See Module 5, phrase 3.) Problems within the control of the organization are identified, their causes investigated, and their relative importance decided. Problems that are not created by or cannot be solved by the organization staff are referred to higher levels, if this is possible. Once again, the emphasis should be on problem areas where motivating discrepancies exist between crucial areas of organizational functioning and the ideal standard of comparison.

THINGS THAT *SHOULD* HAPPEN

1. System leaders identify problem areas. The systemic diagnosis may help to focus attention upon the weaker areas in organizational functioning and stimulate discussion of the systemic problems facing the organization. As at the work-group level, this process may take one of two directions. System leaders may be able to define a problem vaguely, e.g., "communication is poor," in which case they should be encouraged to get more specific. On the other hand, the diagnosis may generate discussion of several specific incidents and examples, e.g., "We never wrote down that decision," in which case they should be encouraged to identify the more general problem. Both kinds of problem definition should take place. The general description provides a frame of reference; the specific examples clarify the problem.

2. The causes of the problems should be explored. Is a problem being created by a lack of skills or information? A conflict of values? A constraining situation? The source of the problem will have implications for later phases of the development effort when activities for solving the problems are being planned. Therefore, the statement of a problem should include *where* and *why* the problem arises and *who* is affected by the problem.

3. If more information about problems and their causes is needed from

people not present at the meeting(s), the system leaders should design and carry out a plan for collecting this additional information. Such a plan might include interviews with a sample of people lower in the organization, meetings with groups of these people, or small task forces designated to investigate various aspects of problems indicated by the systemic diagnosis through observation, interviews, questionnaires, or meetings. The actual data collection might be carried out by the system leaders themselves, other people in the organization hierarchy, the consultant, a special outside group, or some combination of the above.

4. The leader of the meeting should keep a record of the problems and their causes as identified.

5. After problems have been defined and listed, the system leaders should group together problems that overlap; that is, problems that are closely related or that focus essentially on the same area should be put together under a more general heading. This step will lessen the chances that small parts of one general problem will be solved separately in later phases instead of planning a set of activities designed to solve the whole problem in the very best way possible.

6. When step five is completed, the system leaders should separate those problems the organization can solve from those over which it has no control. When a problem is outside of the organization's control, the organization head may want to refer the problem to his or her superior for consideration.

7. The system leaders should then decide which problems within their control should be solved first, second, etc. Criteria that might be used in making these decisions include the ease with which the problem can be solved, the number of people, departments, etc., affected by the problem, its effect upon performance, and the motivation of people to work on the problem.

8. The leader of the meeting should focus attention on and encourage high priority for those problems that may be solved in a reasonable amount of time without requiring resources (such as skills and money) that the organization cannot obtain. He should do this because it is important to maintain a motivating discrepancy between how the organization functions now and the standard with which it compares itself. A huge problem whose solution requires several months and unobtainable resources would reflect too large a discrepancy to work with. Solving more manageable problems first may lessen the discrepancy enough to motivate people to work on problems that were previously unreachable.

THINGS THAT *MIGHT* HAPPEN

1. The meeting may be slow in starting. People may not be sure what to do first.

Info:	**how systemic prob-ident. fits in effort;**
Skills:	**encouraging the leader to make a suggestion; posting**

2. System leaders may not want to be involved in survey-guided development. They may only be going through the motions because they feel they have to.

Info:	**goals of the effort; benefits of survey-guided development;**
Skills:	**dealing with resistance**

3. The system leaders may think that the survey data do not accurately reflect how the organization functions.

Info:	**source of the data; Survey of Organizations;**
Skills:	**dealing with resistance; collecting additional data;**

4. The system leaders may say "Compared to other organizations, we don't have any problems." They may be trying to avoid confronting some issues.

Info:	**norms;**
Skills:	**identifying motivating discrepancies; dealing with resistance**

5. The system leaders may feel that there are so many problems that they do not know where to start. They may resist this phase of the effort because it seems hopeless.

Skills:	**prioritizing problems; identifying motivating discrepancies**

6. System leaders may not see any payoff coming from the meeting. They may have other obligations that are seen as more important.

Info:	**how systemic prob-ident. fits in effort; benefits of survey-guided development; short- vs. long-term payoff**

7. System leaders may not understand what a systemic problem is. They may confuse systemic problems with work-group problems.

>   **Info:**   **systemic problem; work-group problem**

8. System leaders may not know how to go about identifying problems and their causes.

>   **Skills:**   **identifying problems; identifying the source of problems; identifying causes of problems**

9. People may tend to blame particular system members for organization problems.

>   **Info:**   **causal model; source of the data**

10. People at the meeting may be afraid that they will be or are being blamed for organization problems.

>   **Info:**   **causal model; source of the data**

11. The organization head may take total responsibility for organization problems.

>   **Info:**   **causal model; source of the data**

12. No one may feel responsible for the problems facing the organization.

>   **Info:**   **causal model; source of the data**

13. System leaders may assume they know what the problems are at lower levels in the organization when in fact, they need more information.

>   **Skills:**   **sticking to the data; collecting additional data**

14. System leaders may spend all their time on one or a few problems rather than trying to get a complete picture of what the problems and their causes are. They may continue to offer specific examples long after a common frame of reference has been established. Or the issue of whether a problem is a problem may continue to be discussed.

>   **Skills:**   **posting; separation of P/I and P/S; guiding the discussion**

15. System leaders may spend a great deal of time discussing problems they have no control over as opposed to focusing on areas they have the power to change. Or they may assume they have no control over

some areas when in fact they could make some changes if they wanted to.

> **Skills: identifying control over problems; prioritizing problems**

16. System leaders may say that a particular problem is unsolvable and should not be recorded. They may sometimes do this in order to bury a problem.

> **Skills: separation of P/I and P/S**

17. System leaders may spend an undue amount of time arguing over which problems have the highest priority.

> **Skills: grouping problems; sequencing; establishing criteria; emphasis curve**

18. System leaders may attempt to find out which supervisors had high scores on the survey and which had low scores in order to reward and punish the respective people. They may want to force a supervisor to share his survey results with them, describe his work-group meeting in detail, or share the specific problems identified. Actions like this might violate confidentiality of the survey data.

> **Skills: confidentiality; problem list integrations**

19. System leaders may speculate that problems exist in areas about which they have little or no information. This may reflect a need to collect more information; on the other hand, it may represent an effort to avoid discussing problem areas indicated by the data.

> **Skills: sticking to the data; collecting additional data; dealing with resistance**

20. Personality conflicts may arise. One person may constantly interrupt another, ignore what the person has said, or be even more openly hostile. If this conflict is interfering with the progress of the meeting, an intervention by the consultant may be necessary.

> **Skills: handling conflicts and misunderstandings; staying task-oriented**

21. System leaders may get involved in such a heated argument that they are no longer listening to each other. The true issues may get lost.

> **Skills: sticking to the data; summarizing; handling conflicts and misunderstandings**

22. The meeting leader may dominate the meeting, rather than lead it. He may be quick to dismiss problems as unimportant, post problems only if he agrees that they are problems, or list everything he thinks is a problem first.

> **Skills: gatekeeping; separation of P/I and P/S; encouraging participation**

23. The system leader may want the consultant to make decisions for them, or organize problem-identification activities.

> **Skills: clarifying consultant's role**

24. The project coordinator or other key people may be leaving the organization soon. This may make system leaders wonder whether their efforts to identify problems with the present people are worthwhile. They may feel that the replacement will want to do things differently.

> **Skills: identifying the source of the problem; identifying control over problems; dealing with resistance**

Procedural Option

Meetings of system leaders to identify systemic problems may take place *before* or *after* work group feedback meetings have begun. There are advantages, however, to having meetings for identifying systemic problems after the system leaders have had their own work-group meeting. First, it may be easier for them to separate their own work-group problems from broader, systemic problems. Because they will have a good idea of the problems affecting their own work groups, they may be more ready to pay equal attention to problems regardless of where the problems originate. Second, the leaders may have been offered information about problems experienced by work groups lower in the organizational hierarchy. This information might make the systemic diagnosis more concrete for them.

What if a Consultant is Not Available for This Phase?

Although it is very desirable that a consultant be available to aid system leaders in identifying systemic problems, there may be some cases when this is not possible. The following mechanisms are offered as alternative ways of helping system leaders in identifying systemic problems:

1. The consultant might hold a training session for the system leaders sometime before they are ready to begin this phase.
2. The consultant might prepare a guide for the leader of the meeting, explaining the steps involved, what to do, what might happen, procedural options, skills needed, etc.
3. The consultant might discuss with system leaders what should happen when identifying systemic problems and how it should happen sometime before this phase begins.
4. The consultant might run through a sample problem-identification process as a sort of crash training program.
5. The consultant and the organization's project coordinator might discuss how this phase is going from time to time.
6. The consultant might establish links between the project coordinator and consultants who can give help by phone, mail, or short visits.

Key Points in Systemic Problem-Identification

This module focused on how to make use of the systemic diagnosis in identifying systemic problems. Several key points emerge:

- Systemic problems are problems that cut across functions, hierarchical levels, survey indices, and time.
- Problems are caused by a deficiency in one or more of four areas: information, skills, values, or situation.
- A systemic problem, when fully defined, describes the ineffective behaviors/policies/conditions, the reasons why the problem persists (i.e., its causes), its pervasiveness, where it originates, and where it impacts.
- The active involvement of organization leaders is essential.
- The consultant must guide the problem identification process to insure that the real systemic problems receive attention.

Module 8
Solving Systemic Problems

Formulating an accurate description of systemic problems is an important objective of survey-guided development. The process of diagnosing the weaknesses and strengths in organizational functioning is, in and of itself, a constructive intervention in the ongoing activities of the organization. It is crucial, however, that these problems be solved if organization members are to trust the intentions and commitment of the leaders.

As noted in Module 7, systemic problems are those that affect many people, hierarchical levels, and functional areas of the organization. This means that the presence of serious systemic problems is likely to affect the whole organization adversely. System leaders influence organizational climate more than any group of people below them in the organization. Because of this, it is important that the system leaders be actively involved in this phase of the development effort. If proposed changes do not have their commitment and support, the changes may never occur. On the other hand, if system leaders actually design and help to implement solutions to systemic problems, change will have already begun. When systemic problems are being solved, the likelihood is greater that solutions to work-group level problems will be successful.

PROBLEM SOLVING AT THE SYSTEM LEVEL

A note about format: in the following pages, five kinds of information are given. First, there are some general notes about systemic problem solving.

After this general information, there is a list of events that should occur during a problem-solving meeting. You might consider these guidelines for a good session. If they do not occur, the consultant should try to judge whether the activities that are occurring are appropriate, given the objectives of the meeting. If they are not, you should be prepared to step in and guide the meeting in the appropriate direction.

Then, a second set of events is listed; namely, those things that might occur during a problem-solving session and that need to be dealt with if they do. You might consider these problems that should be avoided in a good meeting. If these things happen, the consultant should once again step in and provide the necessary information or use the necessary skills to keep the meeting in a more productive vein. After each such item, one or more key phrases will be listed (e.g., **consultant role; dealing with resistance**). These key phrases refer to the techniques, that is, the information and skills that the consultant might use in the situation described. These techniques are defined and illustrated in Module 9 and can be referenced by their key phrases.

Fourth, some mechanisms are suggested that might enable system leaders to hold these sessions in the event that a consultant is not available to guide the process.

Finally, the major issues in this section are highlighted by a listing of key points.

GENERAL OVERVIEW

Once a list of systemic problems, their causes, and their relative importance has been formulated, system leaders should focus on solving the problems. The outcome of meetings during this phase should be workable, agreed-upon solutions that take care of the problems at hand without creating new ones. Solutions should be stated in terms of the specific action steps involved, the people responsible, and the proposed time frame for implementing each step, as well as in terms of the more general strategies adopted.

System leaders should choose solutions on the basis of how well the proposed corrective activities will tackle the identified problems and their causes. If action steps are planned without tailoring them to meet the diagnosed needs of the organization, the solution may be ineffective or even detrimental.

In establishing the time frame for the solutions, careful attention should be given to the order in which action steps will be implemented. If one part of a problem should be solved before another part can be worked on, the action steps should be planned and sequenced accordingly.

A designated organization leader or the consultant himself may lead the meetings held to solve systemic problems. In any case, the consultant intervenes when the discussions are not progressing or when they are moving in a counter-productive direction. However, the consultant should not be so active that he or she creates a situation where the system leaders see the consultant as responsible for designing and implementing the solutions. The primary responsibility for this belongs with the system leaders, while the consultant helps them primarily through his transducer role. (See Modules 1 and 9 for a description of the consultant's transducer role. The key phrase to refer to in Module 9 is **Info: consultant role.**)

THINGS THAT *SHOULD* HAPPEN

1. System leaders should solve problems systematically. Following a set of guidelines often helps the problem-solving process move more smoothly and efficiently. The problem-solving steps described in Module 7 provide such a set of guidelines.

2. When restating the problem to be solved, system leaders should include:

   a. The content area of the problem: Is the problem in communication flow? Supervisory goal emphasis? Peer team building?

   b. The cause of the problem. Do people lack necessary information about what makes organizations effective? Do they lack skills? Do they hold values that are incongruent with those related to effective functioning? Do they work in a constraining situation? (See Modules 7 and 9 for a discussion of the causes of problems. The key phrase to refer to in Module 9 is **Skills: identifying causes of problems.**)

   c. Where in the organization the problem originates. Does the problem begin with the top managers? At the department head level? At the division head level, etc.?

   d. Whom the problem affects and the pervasiveness of its effects. Does it affect the whole organization? Several hierarchical levels? People in one department, etc.?

   This information should have been gathered when the problems were originally defined.

3. When system leaders are generating, evaluating, and choosing solutions for problems, it is essential that corrective activities focus upon the appropriate problem areas (i.e., content; see item 2.a). Attention should also be given to the primary "target" of the corrective activities; that is, will the solution focus upon primarily providing information? Skills? Changing the situation? A "change in values" has not been included as a possible primary target of corrective activities because the authors know of no techniques for chang-

ing values *directly*. Values are usually changed indirectly by providing new information, new skills, or by changing the situation in which a person functions.

4. Given the particular problem being solved and its causes, system leaders should decide whether it would be most effective to:

   a. Eliminate the cause of the problem *directly*;

   This approach would mean choosing corrective activities that have the same primary "target" (i.e., information, skills, situation) as the cause of the problem (i.e., lack of information, lack of skills, constraining situation).

   or

   b. Eliminate the cause of the problem *indirectly*.

   This approach would mean choosing corrective activities with a primary "target" (i.e., information, skills, situation) different from the cause of the problem (i.e., lack of information, lack of skills, constraining situation, incongruent values). The indirect approach must be used when a problem is caused by incongruent values, since no change techniques have "a change in values" as their primary target.

   An example may help to clarify the difference between these two approaches:

   > A problem is uncovered in the area of peer team building. Its cause is a situation in which the structure of the organization encourages supervisors to work with subordinates in one-to-one relationships. Because of this structure, subordinates never see or work with one another. Using the direct approach, the existing structure (i.e., the situation) might be changed to one that utilizes work teams, thus encouraging more contact among subordinates. Using the indirect approach, supervisors might be given information about the benefits of teamwork and/or might be given skill training in how to encourage teamwork. It would then be up to the supervisors to bring about a change in the organizational structure.

   Choosing one approach over the other will depend partly upon the relative practicality and acceptability of the potential corrective activities called for by each of the two approaches.

5. When more than one problem is to be solved, or when a single problem is large in scope, special attention should be given to implementing action steps in the appropriate order. Some problems, or aspects of a problem, need to be worked on before others can be solved. Some action steps have to be taken before others can be attempted.

Case example:

> *The problem:* The systemic diagnosis and additional interviews indicate a problem. First-line supervisors in several functional areas are seen by their subordinates as ineffective in managing and coordinating people. They focus on technical requirements of the job without helping or teaching subordinates to coordinate their activities, anticipate and adapt to peak loads, crisis situations, etc.
>
> *Causes of the problem:* (1) First-line supervisors lack skills in the area of managing people. (2) Second-line supervisors think that first-line supervisors should focus on the technical aspects of their jobs, and that personnel and coordination problems should be handled at the higher level. First-line supervisors are expected to behave accordingly. Therefore, the second-line supervisors hold values incongruent with those necessary for the first-line supervisors to be effective. Furthermore, these values create a constraining situation in which, even if they had the skills, first-line supervisors could not behave effectively.
>
> *Sequencing action steps:* It is obvious that first-line supervisors need skill training in managing people. However, if they were merely given this training, they would probably not change their leadership styles on the job because their superiors would still be "sending messages" that say "Managing people is not your territory." Therefore, before giving first-line supervisors training, their situation (i.e., the values of their supervisors) needs to be changed. This might be accomplished indirectly by (1) providing information for second-line supervisors about the negative consequences of the leadership style presently practiced at the first-line supervisory level and (2) teaching them how to send the appropriate 'messages' to their subordinates.

Thus, action steps must be sequenced according to the source and nature of the problem being solved.

6. A change in one hierarchical level or functional area of the organization is bound to have effects on other levels and areas because of the interdependence of roles and functions. System leaders should anticipate the secondary effects of any change and take the appropriate steps to insure that these effects are positive rather than negative.

Case example:

> The example in item 5 described a set of corrective activities for upgrading the leadership skills of first-line supervisors. Suppose that the values of the second-line supervisors change, and that first-line supervisors receive skill training and become more active and effective in managing their people. What might happen?
>
> Second-line supervisors have had a part of their jobs removed—they no longer handle personnel and coordination problems of the nonsupervis-

ory people. This might make them feel that their territory has been invaded, their jobs narrowed, and their roles made ambiguous. Unless something is done to correct these conditions, a new problem at the second-line supervisory level may arise. Therefore, a true solution to the original problem would include working with at least second-line supervisors and first-line supervisors to redefine their roles.

THINGS THAT *MIGHT* HAPPEN

1. The discussion may jump from one topic to another without focusing on one problem long enough to accomplish anything.

   Info: **problem-solving steps;**
   Skills: **prioritizing problems**

2. People might not be willing to share their ideas because as soon as an idea is presented, someone begins to give all the reasons why it will not work.

   Skills: **brainstorming;**
   dealing with resistance

3. The system leaders may show low energy and commitment during this phase because they feel that the problems are unsolvable.

   Skills: **identifying motivating**
   discrepancies;
   identifying control over
   problems;
   dealing with resistance

4. The system leaders may feel that their ongoing responsibilities take all their time as it is, and that these tasks are more important than solving systemic problems.

   Info: **short- vs. long-term payoff;**
   how systemic prob-solv. fits
   in effort

5. The system leaders may decide which general strategy they want to use to solve a problem without planning the specific action steps it requires and without assigning responsibility to particular people for implementing the action steps. This makes the solutions ambiguous and very difficult to implement.

   Skills: **planning action steps**

6. The system leaders may decide to implement a solution that directly affects people not included in the discussions, without finding out what implications the changes will have for them. Will the proposed solution solve the problem? Might it create new problems for them?

Skills: collecting additional data;
trouble-shooting

7. The system leaders may plan action steps without considering the effects these steps will have on people indirectly affected by the changes.

Skills: integrating problem lists;
establishing criteria;
trouble-shooting

8. The system leaders may choose corrective activities without considering carefully whether the activities will solve the diagnosed problem. Corrective activities may be chosen, instead, purely on the basis of how easy they are to implement.

Skills: matching solutions with
diagnosed problems

9. The system leaders may want the consultant to run the meeting, make decisions for them, or implement action steps.

Info: consultant role

10. The system leaders may not be aware of the kinds of corrective activities that have been used to solve similar problems in other organizations.

Info: consultant role

11. System leaders may take a cookbook approach to solving problems rather than tailoring action steps to meet diagnosed needs. For example, they may decide to have a week of leadership training or to utilize management by objectives as they are usually run without considering new combinations of activities or modifications of existing techniques.

Skills: matching solutions with
diagnosed problems;
trouble-shooting

12. The system leaders may not plan action steps in a logical, appropriate order.

Skills: sequencing

What If a Consultant Is Not Available for This Phase?

Although it is very desirable that a consultant be available to aid the system leaders in solving systemic problems, there may be some cases when this is not possible. The following mechanisms are offered as alternative ways of helping system leaders to solve systemic problems:

1. The consultant might hold a training session for the system leaders sometime before they are ready to begin this phase.

2. The consultant might prepare a guide for system leaders to follow, which explains the steps involved, what they should do, what might happen, procedural options, skills needed, etc.

3. The consultant might discuss with system leaders what should happen when solving systemic problems sometime before this phase begins and how it should happen.

4. The consultant might run through a sample problem-solving process as a sort of crash training program.

5. The consultant and the project leader might discuss how the phase is going from time to time.

6. The consultant might establish links between the project and/or system leaders, consultants who can give help by phone, mail, or short visits.

Key Points in Systemic Problem Solving

Formulating an accurate description of systemic problems and strengths is in itself, a constructive intervention in the ongoing activities of the organization. It gives organization leaders information as to where they need to focus their development efforts, and it is a prerequisite to solving the problems. This module focuses on guidelines for solving systemic problems effectively. Some key points emerge from the discussion:

- Problems and their causes must be identified *before* corrective activities can be selected. Although this point seems intuitively obvious, it is all too often overlooked.

- Treatments must be matched with problems and their causes. A problem may be solved directly (by utilizing corrective activities with the same primary target as the cause of the problem) or indirectly (by utilizing corrective activities with a primary target different from the cause of the problem).

- Action steps for solving problems should be carefully sequenced since some changes may need to take place before others may be attempted.

- A change in one area of the organization's functioning is bound to have effects on related areas. Care should be taken to insure that secondary effects have positive, rather than negative, consequences for overall functioning.

CORRECTIVE ACTIVITIES

As described in Module 1, a survey-guided development effort includes activities that are undertaken to lessen the discrepancy between actual and ideal levels of organizational functioning. To a large degree, the design and implementation of systemic problem solutions, as described above, are such activities. Occasionally, however, a problem solution requires a more specific intervention, perhaps in the form of a workshop or seminar for certain organization members.

When a more specific corrective activity is called for, care should be taken to insure that it meets certain criteria. First, the activity should be chosen based on the identified cause of the problem. It should be intended to alleviate the cause either directly or indirectly through a predicted chain of cause-and-effects events. Meeting these two criteria will prevent panacea-type corrective activities that operate on the philosophy that "A communications workshop (or whatever) can't *hurt* and it's bound to help somebody" and pay little attention to diagnosed problems.

There are two additional criteria that corrective activities should meet. They should be aimed at an appropriate level both in terms of the organization members who will participate and the degree of skill or information the activity is designed to provide. The final criterion is that the activity be conducted at an appropriate time.

To illustrate these points, consider the case where first-line supervisors lacked supervisory skills, but operated in a situation that would not allow them to exercise such skills, even if they had them, (i.e., second-line supervisors holding conflicting values). An appropriate corrective activity would provide supervisory skill training.

The training should only be given to the first-line supervisors, rather than to a larger range of organization members. Furthermore, it should not be provided until after some other intervention has been made to create a situation that supports the use of such skills, such as activities that give second-line supervisors alternative models for effective leadership and allow them, as well as first-line supervisors, to redefine their roles. Otherwise, the first-line supervisors could learn skills they would be constrained from using, with the probable result of increased frustration and dissatisfaction. Thus, all four criteria for an appropriate corrective activity should be met in order to promote its full effectiveness and avoid possible negative side-effects.

Basically, there are two types of specific corrective activities. First, there are a wide variety of techniques that are currently applied in numerous organizational settings. Such techniques can be differentiated according to which problem source they impinge on most directly—information, skills, or situation. Examples of such techniques would include laboratory training, management by objectives, operations research, process consultation, and team development. For a description of these and other techniques, see Bowers, Franklin, and Pecorella (1975).

A second type of specific corrective activities includes specially-designed treatments that have been tailored to meet the established criteria for a particular organization. Often, they can be adapted from elements of the other kinds of activities with a minimum of effort. Combining segments of pre-existing techniques in order to meet an organization's unique needs may be a more effective use of time and resources than conducting a full-scale intervention technique. Thus, using the systemic diagnosis and problem identification as a starting point, there are many possible corrective activities that can be effectively designed and carried out to bring an organization closer to its ideal level of functioning.

Section IV

Consultant Interventions

Module 9:   Key-Phrase Index: Consultant Skills

and Information

Module 9
Key Phrase Index: Consultant Skills and Information

INTRODUCTION

A crucial part of the consultant's role in guiding the survey-guided-development process effectively is knowing *when* to make an intervention and *what kind* of intervention to utilize. Thus, in parts of the manual focusing on work-group (Modules 4 and 5) and system-level (Modules 7 and 8) meetings, there were guidelines describing the activities that should occur. In addition, problematic situations that might arise during the meetings, and should be dealt with if they do, were listed. Examples of the interventions that should be made in each situation were referenced by key phrases. This particular format was utilized in order to sensitize the consultant to when an intervention is called for and what kind of intervention is needed in order for the meeting to progress as it should. In this module, the interventions indicated by the key phrases are described.

The interventions referenced in the previous modules fall into two categories: (1) those that involve providing *information* and (2) those that involve a *skill*. Furthermore, various interventions are more relevant to some phases and processes in survey-guided development than others. The outline of key phrases on the following two pages is included in order to facilitate the use of this module as a general index.

Outline of Key Phrases

I. Information Interventions
   A. Survey-guided development (SGD)
      1. Definition of SGD
      2. Benefits of SGD
      3. Goals of the effort
      4. Consultant role
      5. Short- vs. long-term payoffs
   B. Data collection and interpretation
      1. Survey of Organizations
      2. Source of the data
      3. What the data mean
      4. Norms
      5. Value of standards of comparison
      6. Causal model
   C. Group-data feedback
      1. Value of feedback
      2. How one-on-one meeting fits in effort
      3. Group-data-feedback package
      4. How group feedback meeting fits in effort
      5. Work-group problem
      6. Value of group problem solving
      7. Problem-solving steps
   D. Systemic-data feedback
      1. Systemic problem
      2. Value of group problem solving
      3. Problem-solving steps
      4. How systemic prob-ident. fits in effort
      5. How systemic prob-solv. fits in effort

II. Skill interventions
   A. Data discussion
      1. Staying task-oriented

      2. Sticking to the data

      3. Staying objective

      4. Identifying motivating discrepancies

      5. Confidentiality

  B. Problem identification

      1. Identifying problems

      2. Identifying motivating discrepancies

      3. Dealing with silence

      4. Collecting additional data

      5. Posting

      6. Objectifying problems

      7. Separation of problem-identification (P/I) and problem-solving (P/S)

      8. Identifying the source of problems

      9. Grouping problems

    10. Prioritizing problems

    11. Sequencing

    12. Establishing criteria

    13. Emphasis curve

    14. Identifying control over problems

    15. Problem-list integrations

    16. Jumping to problem-solving (P/S)

    17. Identifying causes of problems

  C. Problem-solving

      1. Brainstorming

      2. Establishing criteria

      3. Matching solutions with diagnosed problems

      4. Planning action steps

      5. Sequencing

  D. General skills

      1. Clarifying consultant's role

      2. Dealing with resistance

      3. Gatekeeping

      4. Encouraging participation

5. Encouraging the leader to make a suggestion
6. Guiding the discussion
7. Summarizing
8. Troubleshooting
9. Giving effective feedback
10. Handling conflicts or misunderstandings

The description of a specific intervention can be referenced by locating the key phrase under the appropriate category (Information or Skills) in the pages to follow. Key phrases within each category are arranged alphabetically by the first letter of the key phrase. The following examples illustrate how to use this module.

Assume that you are reading about the problematic things that might happen while feeding back data to a work-group supervisor. (This topic is covered in Module 4.) One problematic situation described is the following:

> The supervisor may deny or reject the data. He may claim that the survey was filled out on a "bad day." He may concentrate on the mean scores rather than on percentiles.

The examples of appropriate interventions you might make to handle this particular situation are listed in the following format:

Info: **source of the data; norms**

Skills: **dealing with resistance**

In order to read the full descriptions of the interventions you refer back to the index in this module. To read about "source of the data," you turn to the Information section and locate the key phrase **Source of the data** in the alphabetical listing of descriptions. In order to read about "dealing with resistance," you would turn to the Skills section and locate **Dealing with resistance**.

Assume that you are preparing to work with an organization in the field. A meeting has been scheduled by you with top-level system leaders to identify system-wide problems. Before attending the meeting you might want to quickly review some of the interventions most appropriate to this phase of the effort. You could look over the outline presented in this module, find the key phrases listed under sections I.D (systemic-data feedback), II.B (problem identification) and II.D (general skills) and refer to them in the index. Using the outline as a key to the index might also be helpful when you want to consider what you could have done differently to handle a situation in a given meeting you have already attended.

KEY PHRASE INDEX

Information

Benefits of SGD: benefits of survey-guided development

The several responsibilities that system leaders have might make them reluctant to devote time and energy to the survey-guided development effort—especially if they are not aware of the potential benefits of SGD.

The potential benefits include:

- A periodic reading of organizational functioning that will indicate human resource management problems
- Training and guidance in how to diagnose and solve effectively a wide spectrum of human resource management problems
- Increased understanding of the ways in which human resource management affects organizational performance, retention, etc.
- Increased understanding of how to improve organizational functioning in the immediate future without sacrificing long-range effectiveness

Causal model

An understanding of the interrelationships of the indices measured by the Survey of Organizations and the way they affect each other in a causal manner is needed to properly prioritize and analyze problems. An appreciation of the causal model will help preclude the casting of blame or assignment of responsibility to limited areas of activity.

Basically, an entire system and its component work groups operate in and are affected by the organizational climate. Supervisory leadership is largely affected by climate conditions. Peer leadership is affected by organizational climate and supervisory leadership, and peer leadership affects group process. This latter coordination among group members affects results such as satisfaction and other outcomes such as performance or efficiency. Understanding these cause-effect relations is important in identifying and prioritizing areas for concern, since problems in some areas cannot be solved until solutions in areas earlier in the causal chain are implemented. The causal model is discussed fully in Modules 3 and 6. In addition, the model can be a very useful way to organize the various indices when analyzing data or feeding them back to work groups.

Consultant role

Organization members will be more committed to the survey-guided development effort if they play a central role in planning and implementing it. The consultant might be fairly active at meetings but should not take *primary* responsibility for any phase of the effort. Generally, more direction from the consultant is needed at the systemic than at the work-group level.

Throughout the effort the consultant acts as a transducer, that is, as an energy link between valid scientific information regarding organizational functioning and change processes on the one hand, and the people involved in the development effort on the other. In Module 1 the transducer role is discussed in more detail.

Definition of SGD: definition of survey-guided development

If organization members are to be supportive of and active in the survey-guided development effort, they must know *what* activities will be included and *why*. Remember to provide only as much information as the client wants and can handle at one time.

Module 1 describes survey-guided development in some detail. *Very briefly*, however, this development approach includes two phases: a diagnostic and a change phase. The purpose of the diagnostic phase is to define problems and their causes and to indicate what changes are needed to solve these problems. The purpose of the change phase is to make the necessary corrections. A standardized questionnaire is utilized to gather multiple perceptions of organizational functioning. By comparing perceptions of how the organization does function with some standard of how it might or should function, the areas needing development become apparent.

Goals of the effort

System members will not be motivated to devote time and energy to a problem if it seems tangential to their primary job responsibilities. A program with a realistic and meaningful goal offers something to strive toward and may become a motivating force.

The ultimate goal of survey-guided development is to achieve effective utilization of human resources by providing accurate and useful information about how an organization does function, how it might function, and how to make the actual functioning more like the ideal functioning. Module 1 is devoted to a general description of survey-guided development and its goals.

Group-data-feedback package

Often when data are being fed back to a work group and its supervisor, a data-feedback package can be a useful tool. Such a package is given to the work-group supervisor and contains many definitions of terms used, information about the items and indices, and explanations of how to construct and interpret data displays. It would be the responsibility of the consultant to develop such a package. Module 3 contains a description of the kinds of things a group-data-feedback package should contain.

How group feedback meeting fits in effort

Since work-group-level data are generated by and are the summarized perceptions of all work-group members, they have the information that may be needed to clarify the survey data. Moreover, since the problems the data may indicate are those perceived by group members, they should be involved in a further identification and solution of those problems. Also the kinds of problems identified at work-group levels will help system leaders make a more accurate assessment of conditions and problems at a systemic level.

How one-on-one meeting fits into effort

Because a work-group feedback meeting is primarily the responsibility of the work-group supervisor, it is important that the group-level data be properly fed back to him. The consultant must help him understand what the data are and are not indicating. You should do all you can to insure his commitment to discussing the data with his group and solving problems as a group. You should help him plan for the group-feedback meeting; adequate preparation for the one-on-one meeting will enhance its success.

How systemic prob-ident. fits in effort: how systemic problem identification fits into the survey-guided development effort

Since system problems affect many people, roles, levels, and functions, solving such problems is bound to increase the effectiveness of the whole organization. Before solutions can be planned, however, the system problems must be fully defined. The systemic diagnosis indicates strengths and weaknesses in organizational functioning and may be used as the basis for problem identification.

How systemic prob-solv. fits in effort: how systemic problem solving fits into the survey-guided development effort

A statement of the problems an organization faces indicates the areas in which adaptations or changes are needed. If the necessary adjustments are not made, organization members might question the commitment of their leaders to improving human resource management practices. The purpose of this phase is to plan and implement a coherent set of activities designed to make the appropriate changes.

Identifying control over problems

It is most productive for any particular group to work on problems that it has the power and ability to solve. Problems that are not within its control should be dealt with by the appropriate groups.

One way of identifying whether people in a group have control over a certain problem is simply to ask them, e.g., "Is this a problem that you as a group can solve?" There may be times, however, when a group underestimates its own power to make changes and you might suggest that the members explore this possibility. It may also be informative to ask a higher level group how much authority this particular group has to make changes of one sort or another.

Norms

Standards of comparisons that are used in examining survey data sometimes take the form of norms. These are the summarized survey scores for a large number of groups that have some common characteristic. The survey data from a smaller group with that same characteristic can then be compared to the norms as an indication of how well the smaller group is functioning. The concept of norms and how they are applied is explained more fully in Modules 2 and 3.

Problem-solving steps

A problem-solving discussion will proceed more efficiently and produce better quality solutions if it is undertaken in a specific series of discrete steps. Briefly, these steps are:

1. defining the problem
2. generating solutions
3. evaluating solutions
4. selecting a solution
5. building action steps

6. planning for review

These six steps are more fully defined, and specific activities are more fully outlined, in Module 5. The steps should always be separate and should follow the same sequence in order to develop the best possible solution.

Short- vs. long-term payoffs

System leaders need to be concerned about the long-range outcomes of their efforts as well as immediate results, since they are responsible for the organization's future effectiveness as well as its day-to-day operations. Activities set up to meet immediate goals or accomplish day-to-day tasks do not necessarily insure the system's ability to function effectively and survive in the long run. It is building in a *capacity* (information, skills, values, situation) to sólve problems effectively that will enable organization members to adapt to changing conditions.

Source of the data

It is critical to bear in mind that the data used in a survey-guided development effort have been generated by the organization members themselves. It is not a case of an outside consultant observing or measuring the organization and providing some summaries of his perceptions. The survey data comprise the perceptions of those within the system or work group. Therefore, if the data indicate a problem, that indication can be tied back to what people actually were thinking and feeling when they filled in the survey.

Survey of Organizations

The Survey of Organizations is a standardized, machine-scored survey that can be administered to all members of an organization to obtain data describing the functioning of organization (or a work group or unit). The data are used by organization members to identify strong and weak areas, so the members can plan and carry out steps to improve weaker areas of organizational functioning. Norms have been developed for items and indices on the survey during the period of its use in many organizations, so that an organization can compare its data with the norms to evaluate how well it is functioning. The survey covers major aspects of organizational climate, supervisory leadership, peer leadership, group process, job characteristics and satisfaction. The survey is comprised of 124 core questions, 86 of which are used to form 30 indices. The indices give information about a particular domain of behavior or functioning that cannot be adequately measured by a single item. Module 2 provides an explicit breakdown of survey items and indices, as well as more specific descriptions of the survey's development and use.

Systemic problem

Systemic problems are problems for the whole organization, as opposed to a particular work group, and as such they cut across functions, echelons, indices, and time. They may be problems that are:

1. Experienced in the *same* form by many people in different roles at various hierarchical levels for some period of time; or
2. Found in *one* form in some groups, that in turn create problems for *another* form to other groups; or
3. Found exclusively in one or a few groups, but where those groups or their problems are so crucial to the functioning of the organization that their problems may be considered problems for the whole organization.

Systemic problems are discussed in more detail in Module 7.

Value of feedback

Organizations and their component parts can generally be described as engaging in activities that are directed toward goals. These may take various forms from specific production quotas to more general goals, like greater awareness and consideration of employee problems and concerns. Efforts toward their goals can be made more meaningful and efficient if feedback is made available. Information about a system's status in relation to its goals can be used to confirm, adjust, or correct its efforts. Thus feedback is an important link in a process of goal-directed activity.

Value of group problem solving

Work-group members may resist spending time and energy on solving their problems if they perceive such an effort as unproductive or inappropriate. It is important that the work group be acknowledged as the proper place for problem-solving activities. This is true for several reasons:

- The work-group members themselves have the best information about the nature, scope, and impact of any problems
- The work-group members themselves have important information about the feasibility of potential solutions

- Problems requiring solutions the entire work group must cooperate in implementing are best solved by those concerned; any solutions that are generated will have greater commitment if they are owned by the entire work group
- Solutions that may be controversial are more likely to be accepted if they are completely understood and not imposed by someone outside the work group.

Value of standard of comparison

While the survey data for a work group or system may be interesting and useful in that they demonstrate *how* an organization is functioning, those data can be even more useful and generate more beneficial problem-solving activity if information about *how well* the organization functions is added. This can be done through the use of a standard of comparison. The various forms these standards can take and how they may be applied are discussed more fully in Module 3.

What the data mean

To maximize the usefulness of the data and their function in a survey-guided development effort, it is important that organization members have some appreciation for the scope and potential impact of the information that the data provide. The data can be examined and understood at different levels, from a cursory look at the raw scores to a comprehensive systemic diagnosis. People receiving data should be given some idea of what these levels are and their implications for subsequent use of the data in problem-solving activities. Modules 3 and 6 give more detailed descriptions of what group-level and systemic-level data mean.

Work-group problem

In contrast to a systemic problem, which cuts across functions and echelons, a work-group problem is one that is internal to a single work group. It need not be unique to a work group; nor does its source have to be within the work group. The main criterion of a work-group problem is that its impacts on and interferes with the functioning of a single group. Wherever possible, such problems should be dealt with by the work group where they exist rather than be taken to the system level. In the latter case, there would be the danger of using too broad a degree of energy and acting on a problem that deserves and needs a narrower focus.

Skills

Brainstorming

Brainstorming is a technique designed to encourage creativity. It is usually used in situations where alternatives must be developed, as in the solution-generation phase of problem solving. Basically, brainstorming sessions follow some simple rules:

- Every member of the group may and should offer ideas.
- No idea may be evaluated in any way when it is proposed.
- No idea is too unrealistic or bizarre to be proposed.
- All proposals should be recorded.

Very often, people cannot refrain from evaluating ideas as soon as they are proposed. Remind them of the ground rule against evaluation and point out that evaluation will be done later. If evaluating still continues, you might introduce a new ground rule, namely that anyone who evaluates an idea must propose a new alternative himself. Group members are usually very effective at policing themselves about evaluation.

Clarifying consultant's role

The consultant's role as transducer and guide (*not* as a group leader) should be clear to organization members. There are several subtle techniques for defining or clarifying your role during a session:

- Where you sit physically in the room.
  e.g., If you sit in the most central position, organization members expect more leadership from you than if you sit in a less central position.
- When you first speak.
  e.g., If you, rather than the group leader, open the session, organization members may assume you will be leading the session.
- How you respond to leads.
  e.g., The group leader asks you, "What's the solution to this problem?" If you suggest the process they might use to solve the problem, you will be seen as a facilitator. If, on the other hand, you are quick to give a content solution, you might be seen as 'the problem solver'.
- How you respond to silence.
  e.g., If you are consistently the one who breaks the silence, organization members will begin to rely on you to direct conversation.

Collecting additional data

A genuine need for more specific information should not be confused with resistance to the diagnostic data or with attempts to avoid solving problems. There may be times, however, when system leaders need more specific information than the survey data provide. This information might confirm or disconfirm the presence of a problem, give leaders a fuller understanding of an identified problem, or suggest implications that possible solutions to a problem might have for various groups of people. The consultant (or leaders themselves) might gather additional information through individual or group interviews, observation, special questionnaires, or records retrieval. Issues of information validity, time and resource requirements, expertise in using the various methods, and potential redundancy of multiple data-collection methods should be considered when selecting the techniques(s) to be utilized.

Confidentiality

At the outset of the survey-guided development effort, it is essential that a policy be established concerning who will see parts or all of the survey data after they are processed. This is important because all personnel who provide information about their work settings, group members, and supervisors, should know what will be done with this information. Also, supervisors and system leaders who feel responsible for their work groups or departments should know what will be done with the data describing their units. When a policy is in place and is made known from the beginning, all personnel may be assured that people outside of the designated recipients will not see any data without their knowledge and consent. Given this assurance, system members can productively use the data to pinpoint problem areas and improve group or system effectiveness.

So that you and system leaders can outline such a policy, you should provide general guidelines concerning who should and who should not receive various units of data. For example, group members should receive their group's data through their supervisor. Groups should not be pressed to share or compare data with other work groups without the knowledge and consent of all group members. Module 3 provides further information on confidentiality of work-group data. At the systemic level, the policy on who should see the data is based mainly on the extent to which recipients are in a position to implement and guide system-wide changes. The recipients will therefore largely include system leaders. Whether individuals outside the organization will see systemic data should also be determined. The notion of confidentiality of systemic data is further explored in Module 6.

Once a policy of confidentiality has been set up, your job is to make sure that it is not violated in any way. As the activities of survey-guided development progress, system members, either in their enthusiasm or due to resistance regarding their own data, may request to see data that should not be disclosed to them. You should remind them of the policy and reasons why it was set up. You may also suggest that their own data in combination with the norms gives them extensive information to assess and make improvements in their group or system. They should be encouraged to make the fullest use possible of this information.

Dealing with resistance

It is not uncommon for people to resist any new program, including survey-guided development. If this resistance is not dealt with effectively—especially in influential groups (i.e., system leaders)—the success of the effort will be undermined. Dealing with resistance requires three skills: (1) recognizing the specific behaviors that indicate people are resisting the development effort, (2) identifying the reasons for their resistance, and (3) taking the appropriate action to reduce the resistance.

1. *Recognizing resistance.* Resistance to survey-guided development may take many forms. First, organization members might question the goals or activities involved in survey-guided development. They may cancel or postpone meetings, resist sharing the survey data with designated recipients, or maintain that a consultant is not needed. Second, organization members might question the validity (accuracy and usefulness) of the survey data. They may contend that the survey questions are not relevant to them, that the scores do not reflect the real state of affairs, that the standard of comparison is inappropriate, or that the survey methodology as a whole is ineffective. Third, they might be unenthusiastic about the survey-guided-development effort. They may go through the motions without really being involved and merely skim over or focus on unimportant aspects of the data. Fourth, they may be reluctant to work on solving problems indicated by the data. They might maintain that they do not have the time to work on the problems or that they cannot or do not need to change anything anyway. Finally, they may maintain that the presence of an outside consultant would make *other* system members suspicious or "uptight."

Since the behaviors that have been described might reflect something other than resistance (e.g., a truly unique or constraining situation), you must be able to distinguish when the behaviors indicate resistance and when they do not. The more reluctant organization members are to examine the validity of their doubts, and the more persistant, frequent, intense, and rigid their arguments are, the more likely it is that they are resisting the effort.

2. *Identifying the causes of resistance.* Resistance of organization members may stem from one or more of four factors: (1) they may have inaccurate or insufficient *information* about the effort; (2) they may lack the requisite *skills* needed; (3) they may hold *values* that conflict with those espoused by survey-guided development; or (4) their work *situation* may discourage them from participating fully in the effort. For example, they may be afraid that the survey results will make them "look bad" and that they will be punished (lack of information); they may not know how to lead group meetings (lack of skills); they may not want lower level organization members to have any voice in how lower levels in the system function (conflicting values); they may have had the survey-guided development laid on them and yet feel that they do not have the necessary authority to change anything (constraining situation).

If you are not trusted by organization members, you may have to infer what the cause of the resistance is. If, on the other hand, you have a good relationship with the resisting members or with a member who "knows the ropes," you might ask directly why the resistance is occurring.

3. *Reducing resistance.* Providing *information* about the effort, its goals, your role, possible consequences, and policies of confidentiality may reduce resistance stemming from organization members' misconceptions and conflicting values about survey-guided development. Some *skill* training or behavior-modeling on your part might increase their self-confidence and ability to participate effectively. Making sure that members are involved in planning and carrying out the effort in their organization might give them more latitude in affecting their *situation*. Further, focusing on problems within their control and where motivating discrepancies exist may make them aware of the less constraining aspects of their situation.

In summary, dealing with resistance effectively involves defining the behaviors that stem from resistance, identifying the causes of the resistance, and *then*, taking the appropriate actions to reduce the resistance.

Dealing with silence

It is not uncommon for a group discussion to fall into periods of silence. The first thing you should do is to try to understand why the silence has descended. It may be because people are thinking about an issue or problem; in such cases the silence should be encouraged and not cut off. At other times, the silence may indicate that people are waiting for guidance. In these situations, the silence should be broken by a remark that will lead to more discussion, such as "If that's all on this point, let's move on to the next one." Sometimes people may be silent because they do not feel free to participate. Some comment should be made that will clearly invite them to speak, such as "What do you think the data indicate?" or "Can anyone think of an example of this problem?" Finally, silence may be a sign of resistance; the discussion under **dealing with resistance** in this section offers some useful ideas of what to do in such a situation. It is important that someone other than the consultant break the silence whenever possible. Otherwise, if you always do it, you will soon be seen as responsible for the discussion.

Emphasis curve

When a group or organization members cannot agree upon a course of action after discussing and weighing the relevant factors, the consultant may want to suggest that they use a structured decision-making technique called the emphasis curve (see Fuller, 1963). The technique is summarized briefly here:

1. The group should list all the relevant alternatives.
2. Each person should compare each alternative with each of the other alternatives and, for each comparison, record his preference scores (1 = more preferred, 2 = less preferred alternative).
3. Then, the members of the group should combine their preference scores for each alternative. The alternative with the highest priority (i.e., lowest score) is the one most preferred by the group.

Encouraging participation

Group meetings may tend to be dominated by the work-group supervisor or organization head. This may occur because meetings are traditionally run by one person. The meetings that characterize survey-guided development activities should be more participative. This may take active intervention by the consultant in a gatekeeping capacity. If data are being discussed or problems are being identified, the consultant can point out the fact that the whole group or whole system generated the data and feel the brunt of the problems that may exist. Therefore, group members are not only entitled to join in the discussion but are actually responsible for what may occur. If problems are to be solved, the cooperation of the whole group is required and so all group members should feel a legitimate right to participate. It may be necessary for the consultant to discuss this with the group leader before or after a group meeting.

Encouraging the leader to make a suggestion

If a group is hesitant to identify problems because they are not sure of how the leader will respond, your asking the leader to identify a problem he sees as relevant might set an example and get the session rolling.

Establishing criteria

When many alternatives are being considered and evaluated, the decision process can be enhanced by taking a few moments to establish some criteria that will be applied to all items. Basically, criteria are standards for judging. One way to develop them is to brainstorm an ideal choice. Its characteristics then become the criteria against which any alternative can be measured. Various ideas will meet these criteria to differing degrees. It is often useful to identify criteria that are crucial and those that would be attractive but not essential. The best choice then becomes the one that most adequately meets the essential criteria and meets the greatest number of secondary criteria.

Gatekeeping

Occasionally, involving the entire group in a discussion requires some active intervention. If some group members are particularly quiet, they may need to be given an explicit opportunity to respond. A comment such as, "We haven't heard anything from this side of the room; did any of you have anything to add?" makes it clear that those particular members are invited to contribute. Of course, a response should not be *demanded*; they should feel free to say nothing if they wish. There are other situations where a few group members dominate the discussion. It may be necessary to momentarily close off their remarks and invite comments from other members. This may especially be needed when one or two people continue to discuss an issue long after the larger group's interest in it has waned.

Giving effective feedback

Feedback can be a useful tool in helping a person or group to improve or maintain its level of performance. In a survey-guided development effort, that performance may amount to leading a meeting, identifying problems, generating solutions, planning action steps, or any of the other various activities involved. The feedback itself may be positive, i.e., about good performance; negative, i.e., about poor performance; or both. Effective feedback should conform to some basic rules:

- It should be given with the intent of being helpful to the receiver;
- It should describe the performance itself rather than evaluate the performer;
- It should be specific rather than general and include examples of the performance;
- It should only be given about something the receiver has the power to alter;
- It should be given directly to the person who observed the performance and at a time when the receiver is ready to accept it.

Grouping problems

Disagreements about the priority of some problems over others might arise if several problems listed highlight different aspects of one important area. It is not efficient to argue about which particular part of one problem should be addressed first. Therefore, problems that pertain to slightly different aspects of the same basic issue should be combined and included under a more general heading (e.g., supervisory work facilitation). Grouping problems in this way lessens the chances that smaller, overlapping parts of one larger problem will be solved separately, and thus less efficiently, in later phases. Furthermore, addressing smaller parts of a larger problem does not insure that the larger problem will be dealt with—the whole may be greater than the sum of its parts.

Guiding the discussion

When a discussion is unnecessarily lengthy and detailed or is irrelevant to the main topic being considered, the consultant should shift the focus of conversation. This may be accomplished by:

1. Making a process comment, such as "I think we're straying from the most important issue. We were talking about . . .";
2. Highlighting the main points that have been made and suggesting that the group move on to the next agenda item;
3. Actively changing the topic of conversation.

Handling conflicts and misunderstandings

In a discussion, people may tend to approve or disapprove of what is being said before they really understand what another person is saying or the frame of reference he is using. If you sense that this is occurring, i.e., that people are simply talking past each other, stop the discussion for a moment and institute the following rule, first developed by Carl Rogers and often called "Rogers' Rule":

> Each person can state his opinion only *after* he has first restated the ideas and feelings of the previous speaker accurately and to that speaker's satisfaction.

This can be a very effective process for improving communications and relationships with others. Very often apparent conflicts disappear once a frame of reference has been clarified. Sometimes, however, after carefully checking understanding, it becomes apparent that the differences among the people involved are real. You must decide whether the time should be taken to work through the disagreement on the spot. This may be necessary if you sense that the meeting will not progress very effectively if a conflict is suppressed rather than dealt with. At other times, though, it may be possible to put off an argument until later, especially if only two or three people are in conflict and the rest of the group would like to proceed.

In those cases where you feel the disagreement should be dealt with on the spot, one effective way to start is to identify some overall goals or values that are subscribed to jointly by all parties concerned. Once these have been identified, the present differences need to be reviewed in terms of their potential impact on those common goals. Differences with regard to an immediate problem are often resolved by this process. If they are not, suggest that, for the present, one alternative course of action or position be selected, with a commitment to a later review and evaluation of the outcome.

Identifying motivating discrepancies

The *size* of the discrepancies between an organization or a group as it functions in specified areas and some standard of comparison is an important factor affecting people's motivation to solve problems. Very small discrepancies are often disregarded; very large discrepancies may be seen as indicating insurmountable problems. When presenting diagnostic data, the consultant should focus the attention of clients on areas where *moderate* discrepancies exist. This focus may be accomplished visually (by using appropriate data displays) or verbally (by guiding the discussion of the data). Where all the discrepancies are very large or very small, the consultant should create motivating discrepancies by encouraging the clients to set a more appropriate goal (i.e., reassess the "ideal" level of functioning). For example, if norms are the standard of comparison and all survey scores are substantially below average, encourage the client to aim for raising the survey scores to the 50th percentile—not the 100th percentile. If all scores are at or below the 50th percentile, encourage the client to aim for the 75th or 100th percentile—not an average score. The concept of motivating discrepancies is discussed in more detail in Modules 1 and 3.

Identifying problems

In the problem-identification phase of a problem-solving discussion, the problems that get identified should meet two criteria:

- There should be some supporting evidence in the data; and
- The problem should be defined to the point where the whole group understands the issue at hand.

At the systemic level, some attempt should be made to identify the causes of problems, also. When group members are identifying problems they should provide specific examples of task-related problems. They may start at a rather abstract level using general terms, but should be encouraged to get more specific by citing concrete situations where the problem occurred. Ultimately, there should be two levels of description for each problem: a general frame of reference and some specific examples. Once these two levels are reached, the discussion should move on to a new issue, rather than continue on and on with more examples of the same thing. Although it is not necessary for the entire group to agree that a problem exists, there should be some commonality to the problem, so that the group does not spend its energy on a series of individual pet peeves.

Identifying the source of problems

Identifying the source of a problem means establishing *where in the organization* the problem originates, and should be distinguished from identifying the cause of a problem (lack of information or skills, incongruent values, constraining situation) and the part of the organization where the problem makes its greatest impact. The source may be one or a few key persons, a functional area or hierarchical level in the organization, or the super-system of which the organization is a part.

The survey data may provide an indication of where a problem originates. Look for the level at which organizational climate scores begin to drop. Very often the source of problems in leadership and group processes is the level *above* the one where climate scores begin to fall. This flow of events is explained in more detail in Module 6 when the causal model of organizational functioning is described.

Jumping to P/S: Jumping to problem solving

Occasionally during the problem-identification phase, a group's enthusiasm may wane or it may become disillusioned about all the problems it has. One way to overcome this and generate some motivation for continuing later problem-identification is to move directly to the problem-solution phase without identifying all the group's problems. This departure in format should be clearly identified. The group should be asked to name the problem that it thinks could be solved most feasibly. It may be necessary for the consultant or supervisor to suggest one. The six steps of problem-solving could then be followed for that problem. Sometimes, if time allows, the group can return to problem-identification at that same meeting. At other times, it may be necessary to share reports on how the first solution was implemented before identifying more problems.

Matching solutions with diagnosed problems

If corrective activities are not appropriately matched with diagnosed problems, action steps will probably be ineffective. The content or substance of solutions should be chosen on the basis of the content of the problem. Also, the primary target of the solution (i.e., information, skills, or situation) should be considered in relation to the cause of the problem (i.e., lack of information or skills, incongruent values, or constraining situation).

A problem may be solved directly or indirectly. A direct approach involves utilizing solutions with the same primary target as the cause of the problem. An indirect approach means choosing solutions with a primary target different from the cause of the problem. The difference between the two approaches is illustrated by examples in Module 8. When choosing one approach over the other, the consultant and system leaders should consider the practicality of the corrective activities called for by each approach and the reactions organization members are likely to have to various activities.

Objectifying problems

Often, as problems are being identified and defined, a group will start to associate a specific problem with certain individuals. These individuals may feel under attack and become defensive. The consultant should point out that the meeting is not intended to lay blame or identify troublemakers, but to define the group's problem and to work together to solve them. Leading the group back to its data will help shift its focus from an individual to the whole group.

Planning action steps

Planning action steps to solve a problem is not a matter of simply choosing a general change strategy. It includes defining:

- The specific actions to be taken;
- The particular people who will be responsible for each step; and
- The time schedule for when each action step should be taken.

Posting

Any time lists of ideas or issues are being generated that will require later discussion, it is a good idea to post them. This will ensure that no items are forgotten or overlooked in that later discussion. Basically, posting involves making a physical record of a list, ideally in a way that will be visible to everyone. Blackboards and newsprint are traditionally used in posting. Each time an idea is proposed or a problem identified, the person who will post it should repeat the idea, or some shorthand form of it, back to the proposer to check out whether he understands the idea. When some label is agreed on that provides a frame of reference for the issue, it is added to the list. The discussion should then move on to a new idea or problem, rather than continue to center around the idea that has been posted. Very often the supervisor may take the responsibility for posting; he may do this to get a discussion started, and by listing some problems he has perceived or ideas he has had.

Prioritizing problems

Working on one problem area at a time makes it less likely that organization members will feel overwhelmed, and it also encourages them to focus on the same topic at the same time. When there are many problem areas to be considered, the order in which the group will address them should be described. Priorities should be set according to agreed-upon criteria. Some useful criteria might be:

- Importance of the problem area in terms of its impact on organization performance;
- Pervasiveness of the problem (i.e., how many people, levels, functional areas it affects);
- How motivated people are to work on the problem;
- The ease with which the problem can be solved.

If the group is not discussing problem areas systematically, you should intervene and get them to set priorities.

Problem-list integration

The issue of confidentiality is relevant when deciding who has access to the lists of problems identified by specific groups as a result of their feedback meetings. It is quite feasible, however, that the consultant could prepare a summary statement of the kinds of concrete problems identified by groups in various functional areas or at various hierarchical levels in the organization. This summary might provide for system leaders additional, fairly concrete information about the specific problems indicated by low scores in the systemic diagnosis. For the summary problem list to be maximally useful, the consultant should group the specific problems along dimensions similar to those system leaders have identified as problem areas.

Separation of P/I and P/S: Separation of problem-identification and problem-solving.

It is very important that the problem-identification phase be kept distinct from the problem-solution phase. The former is intended to provide a list of the problems that are supported by the data. If solutions are discussed during this phase, two things may happen. First, the group may simply run out of the time necessary to identify the full range of problems or it may overlook some problems because of the combination of activities. Second, if solutions are discussed and evaluated, problems that people think are insoluable will never be posted; these are the very problems that should be shared, so that control can be identified and the issue referred to the proper forum.

One way to insure that the two phases stay separate is to clearly define them at the start and lay some ground rules for what should and should not occur in each. Then if people start proposing solutions or giving reasons why a problem cannot be solved, they can be reminded that solutions are indeed important to group problem solving, but to be most effective, they should be made at the proper time.

Sequencing

Some problems or aspects of problems need to be solved before others can be considered. Some action steps need to be taken before others can be attempted. When planning the sequence in which problems are to be solved and action steps are to be implemented, the consultant and clients should answer the following questions:

- How should people work when the problem(s) are solved?
- What are the specific behaviors and practices that keep people from working in the desirable way?

- What behaviors or practices need to be changed *before* other changes can take place?

Examples illustrating the importance of sequencing problems and action steps appropriately are given in Module 8.

Staying objective

It is very important that the consultant remain objective in meetings. Group members may ask you for your personal opinions about whether problems exist or to take sides in a conflict situation. You should do neither. Rather, lead them back to the data, especially with regard to the norms. Let the data indicate the problems. If you are being pushed to take a stand on an issue, point out that the goals of the meetings are not to determine which side may be right or wrong, but to move beyond that to solving problems.

It should be noted that this objectivity is demanded largely with regard to the content of group discussions. You may have to make subjective decisions about whether and how to intervene in the process of the discussion.

Staying task-oriented

It is important that a survey-data feedback meeting not turn into a gripe session or an airing of personal differences among a few people. Survey-guided development is designed to deal with climate problems at the level where control exists. Likewise, since it is not intended to change personalities, the group should be encouraged to keep its focus on how perceived problems and issues hinder accomplishment of its assigned tasks. Discussions that have begun to wander can be brought back on target with a question, such as "How does that affect how you do on your job?" The response to such a question will put the problem in its proper perspective. Then, if a policy or regulation, for example, does affect a task, then an objection to it raised in terms of its effect on production will have a greater impact on a higher level group than something that is perceived as a more general gripe.

Sticking to the data

When problems are being identified, it is important that they be somehow reflected in the survey data. Requiring some sort of supporting evidence for problems that are being raised will help keep a feedback meeting from becoming a gripe session. Often people will raise as problems some pet peeve or traditional complaint. They should be asked to point to some evidence for the problem in the survey data. If they cannot do so, ask whether it really is a problem. Also, if a discussion has begun to wander off, for example, into a long series of personal anecdotes, asking if and how similar situations can be detected in the data will quickly return the discussion to a better controlled, more task-oriented state.

Summarizing

One way to reduce frustration and to focus a wandering discussion is to review the major points that have been covered. When summarizing you should attempt to integrate previous discussion, in addition to paraphrasing what has been said.

Troubleshooting

Troubleshooting involves having a group of people identify the weaknesses and potential ill-effects of a proposed solution as a means for testing and strengthening it. Ideally, the group of troubleshooters should include some people who were not involved in generating the solution, since its designers may have become overly invested in the particular approach chosen.

THE SURVEY OF ORGANIZATIONS QUESTIONNAIRE

The Survey of Organizations questionnaire is copyrighted in all of its editions. Persons in legitimate, nonprofit research positions may reproduce and use the questionnaire as they see fit. Persons in other positions are reminded that it is only by the receipt of user funds that further efforts to refine and update the questionnaire can be sustained. The instrument, together with a tabulating-processing and diagnostic service, is available from the Organizational Development Research Program, Institute for Social Research, P.O. Box 1248, Ann Arbor, Michigan, 48106, telephone (313) 764-6108. Consulting help in the application and use of the instrument may also be obtained from Rensis Likert Associates, Inc., 630 City Center Building, Ann Arbor, Michigan, 48108, telephone (313) 769-1980.

Although questionnaires of the kind required for survey-guided development can be key-punched to cards, or even hand-scored, the complete membership coverage ordinarily required for effective feedback and diagnosis and the problems of index construction make these procedures cumbersome, expensive, and error-prone. Scoring directly to tape by optical scanning and analysis by computer have proved to be far more accurate and reliable procedures and far less costly. Processing and diagnostic services at reasonable rates have been provided through the Institute for Social Research for precisely these reasons. Of course, to these direct survey charges must be added the other costs of any survey-guided-development effort: (1) the costs of having members spend time completing questionnaires and participate in feedback; (2) the costs associated with maintaining a small group of internal consultants to help in the application process; (3) the costs of external resource persons, both to guide the SGD effort as a whole and to provide specialized inputs as these are chosen by the client system; (4) the costs associated with monitoring and evaluating the effort, regardless of whether these functions are performed externally or internally to the organization.

Bibliography

Bowers, D. G. *Organizational diagnosis: a review and a proposed method*. Technical Report to the Office of Naval Research, 1974.

Bowers, D. G. and Franklin, J. L. Survey-guided development: Using human resources measurement in organizational change. *Journal of Contemporary Business*, 1972, *1*(3), 43-55.

Bowers, D. G. and Franklin, J. L. Basic concepts of survey feedback. In J. W. Pfeiffer and J. E. Jones (Eds.), *The 1974 handbook for group facilitators*, La Jolla, California: University Associates Inc., 1974, pp. 221-225.

Bowers, D. G., & Franklin, J. L. *Survey-guided development I:* Data-based organizational change. (Rev. ed.) La Jolla, Calif.: University Associates, 1977.

Bowers, D. G., Franklin, J. L. and Pecorella, P. A. Matching problems, precursors, and interventions in OD: A systemic approach. *Journal of Applied Behavioral Science*, 1975, *II* (4), 391-409.

Franklin, J. L. *A path analytic approach to describing causal relationships among social-psychological variables in multi-level organizations*. Technical Report to the Office of Naval Research, 1973.

Franklin, J. L., Wissler, A. L., & Spencer, G. J. *Survey-guided development III: A manual for concepts training*. (Rev. ed.) La Jolla, Calif.: University Associates, 1977.

Fuller, D. *Manage or be managed*. Boston, Mass.: Industrial Education Institute, 1963.

Taylor, J. C., & Bowers, D. G. *Survey of organizations: A machine-scored standardized questionnaire instrument*. Ann Arbor, Mich.: Institute for Social Research, 1972.

About University Associates

University Associates is an educational organization engaged in international publishing and consulting in human relations training, research, and education. Along with a growing range of laboratory experiences, workshops, and clinics, University Associates offers custom-designed consultation in the areas of human relations training, leadership and management development, organization development, and community development. Typical clients include business, medical, industrial, governmental, religious, educational, and community organizations.

The University Associates staff of educational consultants, experienced facilitators, and organization development specialists emphasizes an experiential learning approach that utilizes structured experiences, role playing, feedback, and other learning-by-doing techniques that have been shown to result in positive growth for participants.

In addition to the Pfeiffer and Jones series of *Handbooks* and *Annuals*, University Associates publications have expanded to encompass such areas as criminal justice training, management and leadership, classroom education, minority and intergroup relations, growth groups, and psychotherapy. University Associates also offers tape-assisted learning programs in employee and team development, appraisal interviewing, effective interpersonal relationships, listening skills, and health-care education.

Related UA Tape-Assisted Learning Programs

Appraising Performance: An Interview-Skills Course
Norman R. F. Maier

This is a complete course in appraisal interviewing, designed to cover six three-hour training sessions. The tapes demonstrate various approaches to employee appraisal interviews; they also include evaluations and commentary by Maier. A course plan and learning materials (instruments, worksheets, bibliography, etc.) are contained in the facilitator's guide.

2 cassettes and facilitator's guide in 6" x 9" album: $34.95.

Employee and Team Development
(Formerly *Encountertapes*© for Employee & Team Development)
Lawrence N. Solomon and Betty Berzon

This is a ten-session program of structured experiences for groups of eight to ten persons. It is designed for use with or without a group facilitator. The program focuses on the development of the basic interpersonal skills required for employee and team development: self-expression, active listening, ownership of feelings, problem solving, decision making, and giving and receiving feedback.

Four cassettes and facilitator's guide in 9½" x 11" album: $49.95.

The Jones-Mohr Listening Test
John E. Jones and Lawrence Mohr

Providing individuals with immediate feedback on their listening accuracy, this test motivates participants to work on their listening skills. The parallel forms of the test, Form A and Form B, can be utilized in numerous ways, either independently or together, e.g., as a listening instrument in research and evaluation studies. The test is brief, easy to administer and score, nonthreatening, interesting, and easily adapted to many education and training situations.

1 cassette, tests (25 Form A, 25 Form B), and facilitator's guide in 6" x 9" album: $29.95. Extra test forms A or B: 25 @ $3.